ONE RING
TO BIND THEM ALL

ONE RING
TO BIND THEM ALL

Tolkien's Mythology

Anne C. Petty

The University of Alabama Press
Tuscaloosa and London

For Ulrich
my partner in crime, as always

Contents

Preface

MY FIRST EXPOSURE TO J. R. R. TOLKIEN's *Lord of the Rings* trilogy came during the early months of my graduate career. It proved at the time to be the most engrossing, purely entertaining piece of fiction I'd read in a couple of years (and I had dipped into Lovecraft by then). As a budding student of folklore, I sensed there was more to be gained from those three books than several weeks' intense entertainment. Yet it was not until an otherwise dreary winter quarter of Old English that I discovered the author of the essay on Beowulf to be that same Professor Tolkien who had penned my favorite fantasy epic. I began to get really interested.

Some years later, as a graduating doctoral student, I had convinced myself and my colleagues of the depths to which *The Lord of the Rings* could be meaningfully plumbed. The results were exciting to us certainly as scholars of literature, but further, we believed that in studying Tolkien we had gone beyond the end product of the author's genius and had become immersed in the process of creativity itself—mythmaking, if you will. That is the scope of this book: the literary artist as mythmaker. For the insight necessary to the inception and completion of my investigation into Tolkien's great fantasy epic, I am indebted to my mentor and friend Dr. Russell Reaver, who is himself a mythmaker and artist.

My intentions in this book are twofold: to bring before the reader the fascinating process of mythmaking and to intensify his or her awareness of its manifestation as content and structure. Thus the methods employed in this study of Tolkien's fiction will carry the reader beyond traditional literary analysis into the fields of linguistics, folklore, psychology, and sociology. For obvious reasons, then, this is not a book for anyone seeking a general overview of "those fantasy books" the reader has heard so much about lately; but for the serious follower of folkloristic literature, it offers an innovative approach to literary analysis from a broader perspective than is customary. As I open my dog-eared copy of *The Fellowship of the Ring* for the twentieth time, I fully expect to be struck by some further nuance of understanding missed in my last experience of Professor Tolkien's Middle-earth.

ANNE C. PETTY

Introduction

The Road Goes Ever On and On

WHEN I SAT DOWN to write this new introduction, I spent a lot of time thinking about where Tolkien scholarship stands today, especially from the mythologist's viewpoint. Research has changed drastically since the pre-Internet days, when one had to physically visit a library and thumb through the card catalog to know what was being published. Today more information than can be digested in a lifetime is available through computers. Websites for the Library of Congress, university libraries, publishers, booksellers, and literary societies, as well as many sites devoted to anything related to J. R. R. Tolkien, can be accessed quickly and easily. It is not difficult to see that literary criticism on Tolkien's novels, from fannish to academic, is flourishing and that a significant portion of it is sound and well researched. As I sat at my computer, wondering how all that information would inform this introduction, two media events brought it into perspective—one on film, the other on television.

The first occurred during the final week of 2001, when I was sitting in a darkened theater with Howard Shore's Wagnerian-style soundtrack soaring through the overhead speakers and Frodo's final close-up fading to black. "Ring mania" had set in again, thanks largely to director Peter Jackson's widely acclaimed film adaptation of Tolkien's *The Fellowship of the Ring*, the first installment of *The Lord of the Rings* film trilogy. As the house lights came up and the credits began to roll, people were snuffling into their tissues, some weeping openly, but most of the audience remained seated, reluctant to let go of Middle-earth and return to their ordinary lives. Straggling into the lobby, many members of the audience voiced their intentions to see the film again, and if box office figures are any indication, many have.

What strikes me about this experience is the emotional and intellectual force Tolkien's creation continues to exert nearly fifty years after *The Lord of the Rings* first appeared in print. The last time I experienced a Tolkien "tsunami" of these proportions was in the late 1960s, when anyone who was hip had a map of Middle-earth on their door and a T-shirt proclaiming "Frodo Lives." My fellow graduate students in English literature and I carried well-worn copies of *The Lord of the Rings* in our book bags along with the usual course-required texts such as Bright's *Anglo-Saxon Reader* and *Beowulf.* We adopted elvish names for ourselves and used them religiously. In 2002, it is happening again—only this time the Internet's contributions have made the tidal wave even bigger.

What is it about the hobbits, elves, dwarves, wizards, and desperate heroic men of Middle-earth that keeps so many readers (and moviegoers) coming back? When I began doing research for my doctoral dissertation, that was my primary question. Tolkien, besides being an Oxford professor and Beowulf scholar, turned out to be an accomplished storyteller able to sweep his readers along on an epic journey of sacrifice, loss, and redemption. His skill as a philologist was also an important factor in his fiction—his invented elvish languages could actually be parsed and spoken. The depth of historicity that infuses Tolkien's mythology is staggering; the accounts of the ages of Middle-earth in *The Book of Lost Tales,* the tale of the One Ring, and *The Silmarillion* cover several thousand years in overwhelming (some would say excruciating) detail. That Tolkien could create the greater mythic world surrounding the etymology of a simple word such as "hobbit" with such seeming authenticity sets him apart from the many writers of epic fantasy who followed in his wake. As Tom Shippey says in his foreword to *J. R. R. Tolkien: Author of the Century,* "*The Lord of the Rings* has established itself as a lasting classic, without the help and against the active hostility of the professionals of taste; and has furthermore largely created the expectations and established the conventions of a new and flourishing genre. It and its author deserve more than the routine and reflexive dismissals (or denials) they have received. *The Lord of the Rings* and *The Hobbit* have said something important, and meant something important, to a high proportion of their many millions of readers."[1]

Tolkien was not only a gifted writer of character, plot, and description; he was also a consummate mythmaker. At its most elemental level, myth embodies basic human ideals and expresses our deep, commonly felt emotions. The depth and skill with which Tolkien constructs his epic story of the Third Age of Middle-earth lifts it above mere fiction and into this larger realm. As I explained when this book was first published, my reasons for writing it were twofold: first, to acquaint readers with the fascinating process of mythmaking that occurs in the human psyche and, second, to look at the content and structure imposed on literature by this mythic impulse.

My study of Tolkien as mythmaker took me away from traditional literary analysis into the fields of linguistics, folklore studies, psychology, comparative mythology, and sociology. I had a particular interest in comparative mythology, a field where Joseph Campbell remains one of the dominant intellects. I met Campbell in 1970 when I was a doctoral student and attended a university lecture series that included him as a guest speaker. During a brief chat following his lecture, he gave me insight to my dissertation topic—Tolkien's novels read in the light of Campbell's definition of mythmaking. He agreed that *The Lord of the Rings* was infused with the mythic imagination and that my line of study was a valid approach to Tolkien's fiction.

This brings me to the second media event that lends perspective to the ongoing Tolkien phenomenon: the March 2002 rebroadcast of *The Power of Myth*, a six-hour series of conversations between Joseph Campbell and PBS television journalist Bill Moyers. Much of what Campbell had to say about the human need for myth and ritual is as relevant now as it was in 1988, when Moyers, in his introduction to the book that accompanies the video series, offers a response to the question, "Why do you need the mythology?" He observes that the questioner "held the familiar, modern opinion that 'all these Greek gods and stuff are irrelevant to the human condition today. What the questioner did not know—what most do not know—is that the remnants of all that 'stuff' line the walls of our interior system of belief, like shards of broken pottery in an archaeological site. But as we are organic beings, there is energy in all that 'stuff.' Rituals evoke it."[2] We know this is true; it clarifies why Tolkien enthusiasts reread his books and are drawn to watch and rewatch the film version of *The Lord of the Rings*. It is the sense of authentic history, fused with clarity and beauty of expression, that continues to draw new audiences to Tolkien's epic and keeps them coming back to Middle-earth. Like Frodo, the mythic impulse lives on.

Tolkien Scholarship, Then and Now

Literary critics have not been kind to Tolkien. While the animosity has not been directed at the man himself, the so-called arbiters of literary taste have not tolerated his fiction (and poetry), generally dismissing it with an astonishingly visceral vehemence. When *The Lord of the Rings* was first published in 1954–55, reaction from literary critics was swift and merciless. The books were labeled "escapist," "fluff," "facile," "self-indulgent," "juvenile," and "fraudulent." The negative criticism culminated in Mark Roberts's oft-quoted statement that Tolkien's work "is not moulded by some controlling vision of things which is at the same time its *raison d'être*."[3] Such a claim is so stupefyingly oblivious to the completeness of Tolkien's narrative about the struggle between good and evil that one wonders if Roberts had actually finished reading the novels. I think the problem is not so much that the books appeared in the trappings of fantasy at a time when "high literature" was assumed to mean fiction that was modern, introspective, future-oriented, and difficult (replete with intellectual literary allusions) but that Tolkien was not one of the unlearned masses who could be ignored out of hand by academics. He was *one of them*. Tolkien was an intellectual with academic credentials no one could dispute, and this meant he would have to be punished for writing beneath his station, so to speak. His fiction was threatening to literary critics who saw the tremendous popularity of his "archaic" storytelling method as nothing short of a revolution that would undermine their authority.

Even today, modernist critics assault the fictive world of Middle-earth, but much has changed. In the late 1970s, when this book was first published, there were some competent, serious studies of Tolkien, but they were frequently overshadowed by the louder voices of Tolkien detractors. In the 1990s, Tolkien scholarship acquired respectability, and today one can find among Tolkien bibliographies many master's theses and doctoral dissertations, an indication that Tolkien research has become an accepted and viable university topic of study. In a recent collection of essays, editor Daniel Timmons offers the following definition of Tolkien's special brand of fiction: "Tolkienian 'fantasy' is a story set in an imaginative realm in an ancient world, which has the clear presence of the magical or numinous coexisting rationally with the familiar and ordinary; in addition, such a work exemplifies the narrative tone and structure found in the traditional forms of myth, epic, romance, saga, and fairy tale; lastly, the story should attempt to inspire religious joy, wonder, and enchantment in the reader."[4] Viewing Tolkien's work in these terms, we have no difficulty recognizing Tolkien as both a genuine mythmaker for his time and a creator of high art.

By the late 1980s and early 1990s, Tolkien criticism had reached an interesting juncture: the old-guard detractors (mostly writing in the two decades following publication of *The Lord of the Rings*) were opposed by new defenders of the faith who were now armed with respectability and the support of academia. New studies did not shrink from pointing out that much of the negative Tolkien criticism had been the result of two oddly contradictory effects: first, academic critics' ignorance regarding Tolkien's literary specialty (his philological knowledge of language that included everything from immense historical perspective down to localized subtleties, which Tolkien had at his command in mind-numbing detail); and second, the critics' inability to come to terms with the novels' appeal from a completely nonacademic level (i.e., if the masses love it, it must be trash, because it is an established fact that the masses are neither intellectual nor educated). When critics complained, for example, about the inconsistency of Aragorn's dialogue—which ranges from harsh directness toward the hobbits in Bree to the Edda-style prose with which he addresses Theoden and later

Denethor—they were oblivious to the subtle shift in vocabulary, syntax, and rhythm that mirrors the station (or even the species) of the person being spoken to. Even more noteworthy, readers who knew nothing of Tolkien's philological expertise had no difficulty in appreciating the appropriate shifts in speech patterns for each of the characters. This ability to shape dialogue unique to each character is one of the factors that provides depth to the tapestry of Middle-earth and raises Tolkien's fiction to the level of high art.[5]

Several bookstore, television, and newspaper polls conducted in the United Kingdom in the late 1990s in order to determine the five greatest books of the twentieth century consistently ranked *The Lord of the Rings* at the top, and it appears that the thirst for and admiration of Tolkien's created worlds continues undiminished into the twenty-first century. In the information age, the Internet provides access to all things Tolkien, in particular *The Lord of the Rings*. This increases the ability of both the researcher and the devoted fan to satisfy their desire for Tolkien-related information. For readers who want to go beyond the well-documented facts of Tolkien's wartime experiences and career as an Oxford professor of Anglo-Saxon, deeper studies abound.[6]

The Mythic Approach to Tolkien over the Decades

Folklorists and researchers in comparative literature have no difficulty placing Tolkien's fiction, and its accompanying bardic poetry, in the larger category of mythmaking. Tolkien reinvented the iconography of myth for writers of the modern age by giving them new tools in fictional archaic trappings to express the fundamental human experience of courage, sacrifice, and redemption. Tolkien re-created—one could also say elevated—the genre of fantasy fiction into high art. By writing about the fictional world of Middle-earth as if it were retelling the legends of a real but vanished people, Tolkien created a complete mythology that millions of modern-day readers find deeply satisfying. Campbell says in *The Power of Myth*, "The function of the artist is the mythologization of the environment and the

world. . . . The mythmakers of earlier days were the counter-
parts of our artists."[7]

Following the same train of thought, Campbell explains that
the artist-as-hero revitalizes the mythic tradition for his or her
own time, making it "valid as a living experience today instead
of a lot of outdated clichés."[8] Tolkien presented the writers of
the late twentieth century with a wide selection of reinvented,
mythic archetypes and icons, including the desperate quest
(good vs. evil, destruction vs. salvation); a magical object that
embodies or initiates the quest; the wise wizard who oversees
or aids the quest; the reluctant hero who represents the ordinary person (with untapped extraordinary abilities); the hero's
loyal friend and supporter; the warrior king whose true identity
is hidden; magical helpers; and the goddess figure. In the hands
of lesser talents, the use of these archetypes merely paid
homage to and in some cases became blatant duplications of
the fully realized world of Middle-earth and its players. On the
other hand, more talented writers, including Philip Pullman,
Terry Goodkind, Robert Jordan, David Eddings, and Stephen
Donaldson, found themselves liberated to create elaborate fan-
tasy-genre novels without descending into fantasy pulp fiction.

Back in 1970, after convincing my somewhat skeptical doctoral committee—which included professors of British literature, comparative religion, and linguistics—that Tolkien's novels were worthy of cross-disciplinary analysis, I discovered there
were not many scholarly mythology-based studies of Tolkien's
fiction for me to use. There were a few articles in literary jour-
nals and books such as Randel Helms's *Tolkien's World* and Jared
Lobdell's *A Tolkien Compass,* but few studies approached *The
Hobbit* and *The Lord of the Rings* from the context of comparative mythology. By the time *One Ring to Bind Them All* was re-
leased in paperback in 1983, the critical landscape dealing with
Tolkien studies had changed considerably. No longer was it considered faux scholarship to study Tolkien's fiction in depth and
to compare it to many other great works of literature and time-
honored literary traditions. Works such as Edward Crawford's
Some Light on Middle-earth (1985) demonstrated clearly that
there was much to be gained from treating Tolkien's work as

worthy of serious investigation. Dismissal of the books as "lightweight fantasy" was no longer accepted. The newer literati were now turning every sentence, every poem, and every plot device inside out to discover how Tolkien had accomplished such exceptional literary, linguistic, and mythological feats. The sweeping rejections of reviewers such as Philip Toynbee, Susan Jeffreys, and Mark Roberts would no longer go unchallenged.

Researchers in many related fields also find much to admire and study in Tolkien's work. Current criticism includes books recognized for their value to Tolkien scholarship. Thoroughly reasoned and well-written volumes by Verlyn Flieger and Shippey have begun to fill the void. It is widely accepted today that the story of Middle-earth is an exceptional literary embodiment of the deeper mythic imagination, delivering an entire world complete with a three-thousand-year history that incorporates numerous human and nonhuman species and their evolving languages. All this is expressed with such exquisite detail that it becomes immediately accessible and believable— what Shippey refers to as Tolkien's skill at infusing his fiction with "mythic timelessness."

Myth-oriented studies of Tolkien have reached out in interesting and stimulating directions (many are listed in the expanded bibliography at the end of this volume). Two essays found in the collection *J. R. R. Tolkien and His Literary Resonances* illustrate this diversity. C. W. Sullivan III, in "Tolkien the Bard: His Tale Grew in the Telling," uses Theodore Andersson's work on the Icelandic sagas as his model for presenting a folklore-based analysis of Tolkien's use of "story," that is the theme and variations of the bardic tradition.[9] George Clark argues convincingly, in "J. R. R. Tolkien and the True Hero," that Tolkien's twist on the "heroic ethos of the old Germanic world" ultimately places Samwise Gamgee as the real hero who emerges at the end of the quest to save Middle-earth.[10]

Inevitably, larger considerations of the mythic imagination and its expression in literature must involve Campbell, both for a fundamental understanding of what compels a writer to turn to myth as the structure that informs his or her fiction and for a true sense of the essential value of myth to the human psyche.

In *The Power of Myth* video series, Campbell states, "I think of mythology as the homeland of the muses, the inspirers of art, the inspirers of poetry."[11] That Tolkien mined this vast repository of archetypes with skill and vision is now recognized among recreational readers and academic critics alike.

Looking at Tolkien through the Lens of Mythology

The structure and content of world mythology have inspired literary artists throughout history and especially writers in the twentieth and twenty-first centuries. Myth-based literature, however, is somewhat different from fantasy-based literature, and this distinction needs to be made. Since the initial publication of *The Hobbit* and *The Lord of the Rings*, fantasy fiction has flourished. Much of this fiction includes novels structured with what have now become the essential elements of the genre— the wise old wizard, a talisman or object of great power (with the potential for great good or great evil), an impossible quest with a hero willing (or forced) to take it on, and a world in peril, all a debt to Tolkien's work. However, mere fantasy is not true mythmaking in Campbell's sense of the word. The mythos of a culture (or fictional world) is the pattern of basic values and attitudes of a people as transmitted through their art and ritual. The depth to which Tolkien reveals the mythos of Middle-earth constitutes authentic mythmaking. In the creative act of mythmaking, the mythos of the literary work—or the pattern of basic values and attitudes of a people—is transmitted through art and ritual.

Yet labeling a piece of fiction "myth-based" must go further than just finding the surface plotlines or character similarities evident in known myths. Rather, it is the deep structure, the mythos of the created world, that the scholar of comparative literature and mythology seeks to find in fiction. For the purpose of the present book, my excavation of the mythical structure of *The Lord of the Rings* has employed the tools of Vladimir Propp (the structure of folk narratives and fairy tales), Claude Lévi-Strauss (the paradigms underlying all classic myths of the hero), and Joseph Campbell (the creativity of the mythic mind and its impact on the artist). An in-depth look at Propp's three-stage-quest pattern of departure, initiation, and return reveals layer upon layer of "story" growing out of the richly devised history of the Ages of Middle-earth, which culminates in *The Lord of the Rings* (so aptly discussed as interlacing threads by Shippey in *J. R. R. Tolkien: Author of the Century*). Its characters discover their own complicated depths and motivations as the One Ring, and the actual event of the quest, peels away the stuff of which they are made like layers of an onion. This depth of creation was lost on Tolkien's early critics, who too often dismissed his fiction as "archaic" without allowing themselves to see its underlying universal patterns as evidence of higher-level mythmaking.

Applying this three-stage approach to Tolkien's fiction allows us to enter Tolkien's created worlds that standard literary criticism does not encompass. Looking at Tolkien through the lens of the mythic imagination deepens our understanding of his writing beyond its surface literary devices. What Campbell has referred to as the "mythic impulse" in the human psyche applies directly to the evolution and final formation of *The Hobbit*, *The Lord of the Rings*, and Tolkien's posthumously published backstory for Middle-earth, *The Silmarillion*. Investigating Tolkien's fiction via mythology has proved to shed considerable light on the development of Middle-earth as it took shape initially in Tolkien's mind and ultimately in his printed novels. As the creator of Middle-earth—with its intricately developed races of beings, speaking their own languages and referring to their own mythologies and histories—Tolkien fully embodies the role of the modern artist as mythmaker, a role that provides the primary focus for the chapters that follow.

Through this in-depth exploration of Tolkien's role as mythmaker rather than as a writer of stylized fantasy, I hope to demonstrate the value of *The Lord of the Rings* (and by extension the larger body of Tolkien's writings on Middle-earth) for modern readers. Tolkien presents the fully realized mythos of Middle-earth in such a way that readers experience the emotional and psychological process of death and rebirth as if it were real. We come away from the journey changed: we have a new understanding of the ancient paradigms of behavior based on honor, loyalty, fear, bravery, sorrow, and compassion. In this way, the greater mythic impulse shapes the societies we inhabit through the art of the imagination.

Notes

1. T. A. Shippey, *J. R. R. Tolkien: Author of the Century* (Boston: Houghton Mifflin, 2001), xxvi.

2. Joseph Campbell, *The Power of Myth, with Bill Moyers* (New York: Doubleday, 1988), xiv.

3. Shippey, *J. R. R. Tolkien: Author of the Century*, 156.

4. George Clark and Daniel Timmons, eds., *J. R. R. Tolkien and His Literary Resonances: Views of Middle-earth* (Westport, Conn.: Greenwood Press, 2000), 8.

5. Works that bear this out are Shippey (*The Road to Middle-earth*, 1982, and *J. R. R. Tolkien: Author of the Century*), C. W. Sullivan ("Tolkien and the Telling of a Traditional Narrative," in *Journal of the Fantastic in the Arts*, 1996), William Provost ("Language and Myth in the Fantasy Writings of J. R. R. Tolkien," in *Modern Age*, 1990), Katharyn F. Crabbe (*J. R. R. Tolkien*, 1988), and Verlyn Flieger (*Splintered Light: Logos and Language in Tolkien's World*, 1983).

6. Highly recommended are recent collections such as *J. R. R. Tolkien and His Literary Resonances* (ed. Clark and Timmons, 2000), *Tolkien's Legendarium: Essays on The History of Middle-earth* (ed. Flieger and Hostetter, 2000), *Proceedings of the J. R. R. Tolkien Centenary Conference 1992* (ed. Reynolds and GoodKnight, 1995), *Proceedings of the Arda Symposium at The Second Northern Tolkien Festival, Oslo 1997* (ed. Agøy, 1998), and *Scholarship and Fantasy* (ed. Battarbee, 1993).

7. Campbell, *The Power of Myth*, 85.

8. Ibid., 141.

9. Clark and Timmons, *Tolkien and His Literary Resonances*, 13.

10. Ibid., 50.

11. Campbell, *The Power of Myth*, 55.

ONE RING
TO BIND THEM ALL

Prologue

THE REALMS OF FOLKLORE AND MYTHOLOGY have long held fascination for the literary artist, and their lengthy association has been a fruitful one, particularly in our present century. Works such as Joyce's *Ulysses*, O'Neill's *Mourning Becomes Electra*, and Updike's *The Centaur* are probably the first among many examples one may offer as evidence when one begins to consider the growing canon of mythologically based modern literature. These very examples, however, illustrate a distinction too frequently overlooked or misunderstood: that the affinity of a particular literary work with mythology often goes quite a bit further than a discernible parallel with specific myths of the ancient world; it is, in fact, the intrinsic "mythic" structure characteristic of true folklore one discovers in works of modern literature that is most exciting to the student and scholar of myth and folklore. This latter area of investigation has only in the last decade become truly accessible to us, mainly through the efforts of Vladimir Propp and Claude Lévi-Strauss, who have brought to light both the sequential, linear structure of the folk narrative and its latent, paradigmatic patterns. Where once myth was regarded as being a sort of free-form affair in which, as Lévi-Strauss tells us, anything can happen, it is now apparent that the logic of the folkloristic mind is "as rigorous as that of modern science."[1] Twentieth-century man may indeed be the creator of his own mythology, as Joseph Campbell has suggested in his book *Creative Mythology*, and if the artist is a true mythmaker, the elemental mythic forms described by Propp and Lévi-Strauss should be apparent in his works.

An approach of this nature is invaluable to the literary scholar who wishes to deepen his or her understanding of a work beyond its literary devices of plot, character, and theme. The "mythic impulse" in man accounts for many of the subtle beauties of form and content in modern literature, as in the case of J. R. R. Tolkien's *Lord of the Rings* trilogy. A study of Tolkien must come to an understanding of the basic structure of mythological elements, rather than a cataloging of his sources from mythic literature, which, although it reveals the breadth of Professor Tolkien's learning, does not adequately come to grips with the folkloristic structure as it is generated by the mythic impulse. The possibility of a deeper analysis is proposed in Alan Dundes's introduction to the second edition of Propp's *Morphology of the Folktale.* He says, "In understanding the interrelationship between folklore and literature ... the emphasis has hitherto been principally upon content. Propp's *Morphology* suggests that there can be structural borrowings as well as content borrowings."[2]

In addition to the methods of structural analysis employed by Propp, the present study of Tolkien's trilogy also relies on the investigations into mythological systems and the mythic impulse in man conducted by Joseph Campbell, particularly in *The Hero With the Thousand Faces* and his four-volume series, *The Masks of God.* In the latter work Campbell delineates the fourfold functions of mythology and the complex nature of the mythical quest (which is not, as some writers of literary criticism seem to think, simply striving for a goal of some sort). No one has yet attempted to approach *The Lord of the Rings* through Campbell's mythological findings; yet I see it as a method of great promise for the student of literary folklore and mythology. The four functions of myth, according to Campbell,[3] are (1) the *metaphysical-mystical prospect*, which awakens in the individual "an experience of awe, humility, and respect, in recognition of that ultimate mystery" also referred to as the sense of the numinous; (2) the *cosmological prospect*, rendering for us an interpretative total image of the universe; (3) the *social prospect*, which serves to validate and maintain an established order, more often than not, a moral order; and (4) the "most vital, most critical function," the *psychological prospect*. This final function is most applicable to the modern artist as mythmaker, and accordingly, to the chapters that follow, fostering as it does the unfolding of the individual in accord with (1) himself or herself [the *microcosm*], (2) his or her culture [the *mesocosm*], (3) the universe [the *macrocosm*], and (4) "that awesome ultimate mystery which is both beyond and within himself and all things."[4] Campbell has rightly observed that it is no longer the priest who enunciates and validates the mythology of the age; today it is the artist who must assume that role, a burden Joyce's Dedalus struggled with so bitterly. To quote Campbell: ". . . through an intelligent 'making use' not of one mythology only but of all of the dead and set-fast symbologies of the past, the artist will enable the individual to anticipate and activate in himself the centers of his own creative imagination, out of which his own myth and life-building may then unfold."[5]

The immediate problem of grasping the mythic structure beneath the external framework of the trilogy is best solved, we shall find, through a combination of the methods of Propp, Lévi-Strauss, and Campbell. To demonstrate the workings of the mythic impulse in the structure of the trilogy, we must be able to outline the linear sequences clearly, pinpointing incidences of repetition, trebling, and so on, which can be accomplished through the formulae of Propp. But a myth-based study of Tolkien's creation such as I have proposed would remain stranded in the linear architecture if it did not also pay attention to Lévi-Strauss's explorations into the paradigmatic patterns of opposition and mediation. By this widening of the lens, we tap into a more omnibus awareness of the operation of the three-stage quest pattern outlined by Campbell (departure, initiation, return) within the framework of the narrative. An analysis of this nature exposes not only the many-layered structure of the trilogy (too often dismissed as superficial fantasy by readers who do not understand its mythical patterns and functions), but discovers its authentic folkloristic qualities as well, in turn demonstrating the role of the literary artist as mythmaker. In this light, Tolkien's remarks concerning the author of *Sir Gawain and the Green Knight* apply remarkably well to himself.

The author of *Sir Gawain*, while drawing on previous models, fashioned from his own artistry a fresh, new experience out of old material. "He has," says Tolkien, "a special gift for description, and has elaborated the whole setting with a richness of detail unusual in French romance. He handles the story with a moral sensitiveness not to be matched in any of the analogues. His work indeed is not mere reproduction; it is a fresh creation."[6]

Readers familiar with linguistics will be provided with a ready analogy for the type of study undertaken here. The approaches of Propp and Lévi-Strauss are comparable to studies of the surface and deep structures of a language (appropriately, Lévi-Strauss explains in "The Structural Study of Myth" that mythology is language). Beyond these structural investigations, however, lies the final justification for the type of analysis pursued in this book: our discoveries concerning the mythic structure of Tolkien's trilogy must also be set in a humanistic context, a step Propp failed to take in his *Morphology*. That is, we must also indicate the significance of the trilogy's folkloristic origins (and again by this I do not mean specific sources) to contemporary life and letters, which gets us back to the role of the artist as mythmaker. For example, to observe that the books of the trilogy have a cyclic pattern that follows the rotation of the seasons and is symbolic of man's initiation into the good and evil forces of life is merely to observe the surface features of the narrative. Such general analyses can offer only a fleeting surface contact with the mythic origins of these elements and the special influence they command in the artist's work.

To demonstrate the movement from surface to deep structure, we begin with the broadest surface framework available to us: the three-stage mythic quest. Carefully fitted into this structure we find Tolkien's development of three types of heroes, all functioning within the larger quest pattern. At the appropriate point in each of these divisions, I intend to examine the morphological patterns evident therein, to establish the empirical evidence from which to explore the mythic and humanistic implications beneath the surface structure.

In discussing *departure*, we must take into account the mythic origins of the three hero lines of Frodo, Aragorn, and

Gandalf, in addition to other elements from the first division such as the refusal and acceptance of the call to adventure, supernatural aid, and crossing the first threshold. The morphological findings at this first stage of the quest lead into a discussion of the natural world, where we must respond to issues such as the role of nature as a character and motivating force in the events, the necessity and validity of the quest, and the nature of the hero himself.

The *initiation* brings us to the Road of Trials, introducing for our scrutiny the mythic elements of supernatural aid, meeting with the goddess, atonement with the father, and apotheosis, as they are developed in each of the three heroes previously named. The morphological data we receive at this stage illustrates and reveals the manner in which the narrative continually folds back upon itself, as well as how ritual and experience are dramatized rather than explained, again pointing up for us the basically folkloristic nature of the structure of Tolkien's work. It is here that we find answers to questions such as how human experience is reflected in the paradigmatic patterns, what the motivations are that propel the narrative forward, and how nature is immanent rather than transcendent in the universe of Middle-earth. It should become evident at this point that the artist-mythmaker is engaging in a spiritual or personal initiation, as are we who experience his work through its printed pages.

In the *return* we are involved in crossing the return threshold, which concerns us with the ultimate boon of the hero resulting from the completion of his quest, as well as his return, his mastery of two worlds, and society's reaction to the wanderer as he attempts to rejoin the world from which he came. Tolkien skillfully manipulates these mythic patterns and cycles into a finely meshed tapestry of life, which brings us to the question of the "ultimate boon" the returning artist-hero presents to contemporary literature. In the humanistic context, the value of the trilogy for our age is translated in terms of psychic uplift. In Campbell's terminology, this means fully completing the circle of the mythic quest, extending the duty of the returning hero to the role of the creative artist in the fourth function of mythology. The explanation of this "operative value" of myth, according to Lévi-Strauss, is that "the specific pattern described is everlasting; it explains the present and the past as well as the future."[7]

Our understanding of Professor Tolkien's role as authentic mythmaker, by implication, should offer stimulus to the creative imagination in each of us, which is precisely the fourth function of myth mentioned earlier. My final emphasis, then, is on the value of *The Lord of the Rings* as mythology of twentieth-century man's making, recognizing that unlike much of modern literature, which rarely brings the quest myth to satisfactory fulfillment, Tolkien's creation completes this mythic cycle, demonstrating the validity of these primal mythic concepts to our age of the wasteland individual. We are called to the adventure, as readers of a work of fiction and as members of the human community, of responding once more to the mythic impulse.

PART ONE
DEPARTURE

CHAPTER 1

The Mythic Impulse

THE FIRST STEP TAKEN UPON THE ROAD OF DEPARTURE for the quest-journey is always a formidable one, involving anticipation, trepidation, and an odd sense of buoyancy coming from the excitement and expectations of distant lands. In taking this first step we have answered the call to adventure, and the only access to the return threshold is through the mythic cycle of our particular quest. The satisfactory completion of this mythic journey, rich with the ageless symbologies and images residing ever in the wells of man's imagination, fulfills once again the continual desire of the human psyche for unity, wholeness, completeness. It is the age-old process of opposition and mediation, the function of myth observed by Claude Lévi-Strauss in "The Structural Study of Myth"; Joseph Campbell refers to it as "at-one-ment."[1] Further, it is the urge to seek unity and completion in the universe (whether that universe may be found in the external world or within the secret recesses of a man's mind) that we have designated the *mythic impulse*, an inclination followed by priests, poets, artists, artificers, and hordes of ordinary people through the countless years of our human existence.

Recognition and proper assessment of the workings of the mythic impulse are greatly facilitated by a basic comprehension of myth itself and its manifestation as the universal quest. This is particularly true in the case of literary forms, which draw heavily from the resources of the imagination where conscious control is exerted upon the unconscious materials of dream and fantasy. These mythic patterns serve as "a powerful

picture language for the communication of traditional wisdom,"[2] which lies within reach of the literary artist, or more
precisely, the artist-mythmaker, a category that includes
among others Professor Tolkien.

This "picture language" becomes the vehicle through
which myth carries out its function of supplying the human
mind with operative symbols for the dispersement of spiritual
energy from culture to culture and from age to age. The universal myth of the hero's quest is perhaps the most perennial form
of opposition and mediation found in folklore and mythology,
supplying as it does "significant motifs of perils, obstacles, and
good fortunes of the way."[3] *Myth*, we may say, is the transmission of the cumulative knowledge, experience, and universal
truths constant in our human existence, through the consistent
symbologies known to folklore.

The classic stages of the hero's quest agreed upon by most
scholars of folklore, sociology, and comparative mythology—
separation (usually from the community), *initiation* (transition
from childhood to maturity), *return* (knowledge gained)—are
easy enough to recognize in the progress of our own lives. Man
undergoes a continual series of rebirths, moving from one stage
to another, each requiring a set of rituals and guideposts to help
the seeker in becoming aclimatized to each successive plane. At
the end of the progression lies the grail, which the quester,
perhaps sadder but definitely wiser for his experience, carries
back for the benefit of himself and humanity at large. The
completion of the task and its subsequent rewards embody the
satisfaction of the quest. The complexity of this three-stage
quest, which has filtered down through man's existence for
millenia, is as infinitesimal or as cosmic as the imagination
allows. The symbology is remarkably pervasive. We find it in
psychoanalysis in which the emanations from deep sleep rise
through dream to waking and realization, later to undergo
dissolution by returning to the initial unconscious state from
which the journey was begun:[4]

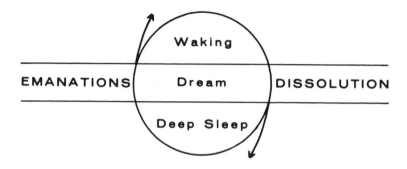

The holy syllable *AUM* serves this same symbolic purpose, in that the element *A* represents the waking consciousness, *U* the dream consciousness, and *M* the deep sleep void of dreams, the seat of potentiality.[5] Here, then, in the waking reality of a work of literature such as *The Lord of the Rings*, we discover the material of dreams and fantasy, while beyond this level exists the most decisive element, the mythic impulse. Is it from Jung's "collective unconscious" as well as from the artist's familiarity with extant mythologies that the consistent folkloristic structure emerges? This relationship between myth and society is a tangled one; yet it remains vital to the energy level and meaningfulness of contemporary life in a relatively godless age.

A new image of man is needed to revitalize our jaded sensibilities, an idea of man as an individual having a unique capacity to surmount pain and despair and attain fulfillment through his own inner resources.[6] Where once the institutions of religion provided mythologies necessary to the life energies of the people, now each individual in society must become his own mythmaker, turning for his inspiration to the artist experienced in making his own way and trusting his inner voice. This is the challenge of our twentieth century to the literary artist. James Joyce took up the gauntlet as he spoke through the mouth of Stephen Dedalus: "Welcome, O life! I go to encounter for the millionth time the reality of experience and to forge in the smithy of my soul the uncreated conscience of my race."[7] Others have followed with equal degrees of success. Yeats, Eliot, Lawrence, Thomas, and Hemingway are among the great names that come to mind, but many lesser known authors such as Eddison, T. H. White, and Tolkien join this mainstream just as readily and often with as much impact.

As was previously mentioned, the way in which the mythic impulse manifests itself in literature is through structural and content borrowings from the body of folklore. The morphology of the basic folk narrative sheds considerable light on the analytic path pursued in this book. Vladimir Propp discovered that there exists an inherent folktale structure based not upon motifs or identity of characters, but upon the various functions performed by these characters. The names and attributes of the characters of myth and folklore may vary; yet their functions and types of actions are constant to the basic material of the folkloristic tale. Thus Propp observed that the themes, motifs, and the characters and their attributes are variables, while the function, or action of characters significant to the unfolding shape of the tale, remains constant or, in other words, is the unconscious product of the deeper mythic mind present in the mind of man. Propp's theses concerning the consistent structure of the folk narrative may be condensed as follows:[8]

1. Functions of characters serve as stable, constant elements in a tale, independent of how and by whom they are fulfilled.

2. The number of functions known to the fairy tale is limited.

3. The sequence of functions is always identical.

4. All fairy tales are of one type in regard to their structure.

Propp discovered that what seemed to make the folktales appear different in structure was the variety of transformations performed upon the predetermined ordering of the functions that must be present. Thus we have a linguistic analysis at work. What appears to be the plot outline of the tale is merely the surface structure, the end product of the various transformations applied to the deep structure elements that are the basic functions performed by the characters. These deep and surface patterns constitute our basic folkloristic-mythic structure. This investigation of Tolkien's trilogy through Propp's methodology illustrates the deep structure produced through the mythic impulse of opposition and mediation; the linear sequence of the multiple quest, charted in this way, reveals the mythmaking process at work. Once the structure underlying *LOTR* (this acronym for the trilogy will be used subsequently throughout the text) has been grasped, the reader can begin to formulate evaluations of the content and its relevance to the contemporary literary challenge discussed above.

A morphological examination of *LOTR* consists of the tabulation of its most elemental units (character functions) and their possible variations as adapted from Propp's list in appendix I of the *Morphology*. They are as follows:[9]

1. The *Initial Situation*, including temporal-spatial designations, family composition or situation, prophecies and warnings, well-being before complication, introduction of the future hero and possible false hero

2. The *Preparatory Section*, containing interdictions, absentations, first appearance of the villain or his agents, interrogation and reconnaissance on the part of the villain, delivery of information to the villain and his deceptions, reaction of the hero

3. The *Complication*, consisting of the first overt act of villainy, the conjunctive moment or form of mediation, the hero's entrance into the tale, the form of his acceptance of the call, the form of his dispatch, the accompanying phenomena, departure from home, the goal of the hero (both immediate and long-range)

4. *Entrance of the Donors*, including the journey to the home of the donor(s), attributes and appearance of the donors, preparation for transmission of a magical agent in the form of tasks, and so on, reaction of the hero, the nature of the provision

5. *From the Entry of the Helper to the End of the First Move or Phase*, which consists of the helper or magical agent, details of the quest or journey, a struggle with the villains or agents of same, marking of the hero, victory over the villain, pursuit and rescue from pursuit

6. *Beginning of the Second Move*, commencing with a new villainy and following the same sequence of functions noted in 3

through 5; this sequence may be doubled or trebled as needed
for the development of the tale

    7. *Continuation of the Second (or Final) Move*, comprised of
the hero's arrival (often unrecognized), the claims of the false
hero, the difficult task or object of the quest, its resolution,
recognition of the true hero, transfiguration, and wedding or
return to society

Moving through these categories of structure, we are concerned
with three elements germane to all the functions just enumerated: motivations, positive and negative results of functions,
and connectives or mediating incidents.

    With the impetus, then, from the mythic impulse, the cre-
ative artist as mythmaker answers the call to adventure, so to
speak, by setting his characters on the road of the hero's quest
and following along himself. Wholly to the point here is S. R.
Hopper's lecture to the Society for the Arts, Religion, and Contemporary Culture on "Myth, Dream, and Imagination," in
which he makes the observation that we are currently living
through "a crisis of the imagination," that is, the imagination
"has now been radically deprived of its familiar patterns and is
thrust back upon the quest for primary metaphor."[10] This idea
offers some explanation for the fact that the predominant focus
of modern literature is stated in terms of the "countermyth" or
antiheroical, seemingly futile projections that deny the value of
traditional mythic images or, more precisely, the traditional
meanings assigned to these mythological images and symbols.
Yet it is only a particular "myth consciousness" that is vehe-
mently protested in the works of Nathaniel West, John Barth,
and others, not the universal myth consciousness we have been
talking about in terms of the mythic impulse; rather it is this
latter realm that provides the very symbols used in the an-
tiheroic works of literature, the same source with new associations attached to its images.

    With the "old gods" swept away in the tide of modern
technology and cynicism, where does that leave us? Once again,
at the mythic source. From the deep wells of the human subconscious loaded with unconscious images and potentialities of
meaning, the artist of our present age is confronted with the

exciting possibility of forging radical new mythologies for modern men. This is distinctly what Campbell refers to when he makes the simple statement in *Creative Mythology* that "the mythogenetic zone is the individual heart." Further, Campbell reiterates Hopper's conviction that the only "honest possibilities" for a mythological revitalization of our culture and, by extension, the products of the literary artist, must occur in a "secular, rational state with no pretensions to divinity" in which each individual is "the creative center of authority for himself."[11]

Hopper projects a hopeful picture for the "crisis of the imagination" on the basis of what he calls "a rebirth of the numinous" or the renewal of myth consciousness in literature.[12] In other words, it is this quest for wholeness, for completion, that forms the "mythopoeic intent" or, again, the mythic impulse. Perhaps it is this lack of the numinous that has proved to be the obstacle in the numerous unfulfilled quests of contemporary literature. In such hollow experiences man does not undertake a quest for the achievement of the goal or vision, but instead for the agonies of the quest, the sufferings of the way; he is the now archetypal fragmented man of the technological age, the twentieth century schizoid. The questers in modern fiction plunge into the search for meaningful relationships, yet cannot carry the search through by returning to the point of origin with new knowledge or a boon for mankind (which includes the seeker himself). With the return of the mythic consciousness or what we may call "that fortuitous thrust of autonomous psychical image formation"[13] that tells the truth in spite of our cynicism, the artist-mythmaker may again infuse the products of the imagination with new meaning and value for a jaded age. The quest of the hero, with its three-stage form of separation, initiation, and reunion, is the "symbolic dimension of human experience as a whole"[14] with its images of death and rebirth necessary to the stimulation of the human spirit.

In order for works of literature these days to supply a sense of unity and wholeness on the mythic, psychological level, authors must be willing to abandon themselves once more to what was known to Coleridge as the *Primary Imagination*. With the guidance of this faculty, we may hope to bring about the opposition and mediation inherent in the myth of the hero quest, the reconciliation of opposites, which, in Hopper's words, "must be radical and light bearing" given the current state of man's sensibilities. With this concept of mediation we return to the observation made at the outset concerning the roles of priest and artist, of the transcendence of God versus the quality of divinity immanent in every man. Hopper's summation is pertinent to the conclusions drawn so far: "It [the traditional theological associations of myth] has yet to come to terms with the Primary Imagination and the transfer of its terms (1) from contests of dualistic transcendence to those of radical immanence, and (2) from the systematics of theo-logic to the open centers of theo-poietics."[15] Moving from general to particular, *The Lord of the Rings* illustrates this satisfactory completion of the quest myth, as a means through which man may confront the ultimate truths of his universe, achieving a sense of integration from that confrontation.

CHAPTER 2

Tolkien's Prelude

FREQUENTLY DISCUSSIONS OF THE CREATIVE FICTION of Tolkien center around the trilogy only, often disregarding *The Hobbit* entirely. Although we may admit this slim volume was, in 1936, a single piece composed by Professor Tolkien to entertain his children, the use it served later in his developing conception of the history of the Third Age is indisputable. For this reason, any serious study of the fictive world of Tolkien must cast a discerning eye upon the original tale of hobbits as an interesting and necessary prelude to the grander work of *LOTR*. The most important demonstration we may conduct here in examining *The Hobbit* is the preliminary use of the folkloristic-mythic structures and functions that make up the intricate fabric of the trilogy. Granted the original hobbit tale superficially appears to be a more comical than serious quest; yet the most profound and ominous elements of *LOTR* are quarried from the foundations of this seemingly lighthearted tale of peril and adventure on the part of a bumbling amateur burglar. The reader should take careful note of the motivations and methods of transition operating within *The Hobbit,* for these are the same techniques employed in the trilogy in a much more complex, accomplished manner.

The Hobbit comfortably follows the three-stage quest of the hero delineated earlier, even though we are more inclined to see Bilbo as a comic figure, even the fool, rather than the hero of the quest. As the opening pages unfold the nature of the quest to reader and fear-stricken hobbit alike, Gandalf the Wizard appears the more likely candidate for hero of the undertaking. This is a deliberate red herring, as we discover when we look closely at the developing hero consciousness in Bilbo, a crucial technique, for it is used again with added dimension in the characterization of Frodo in *LOTR*. We, like Bilbo and Frodo, are not cognizant of their heroic capabilities in the beginning. These qualities develop gradually before our eyes and theirs. Thus while we smile at them as hobbits, we seriously accept their heroic development and the magic surrounding it. Tolkien himself explains this approach in his essay, "On Fairy-stories": "There is one proviso: if there is any satire present in the tale, one thing must not be made fun of, the magic itself. That must in that story be taken seriously, neither laughed at nor explained away."[1]

Tied closely to the developing hero personality in Bilbo as well as Gandalf is this concept of magic. For magic in Tolkien's terms does not mean any cheap, artificial, or external display of trickery and deception, but rather an immanent power of nature that men have somehow lost the ability to tap, presumably forever. Consequently the "magic" of the elves and wizards in both *The Hobbit* and *LOTR* is magic "of a peculiar mood and power, at the furthest pole from the vulgar devices of the laborious, scientific, magician."[2] This understanding of the nature of Faerie prompts Tolkien to look upon the elves as far more "natural" than men, who are "supernatural" if anything, now that they have lost contact with the immanent power of the natural world. Bilbo the hobbit, of a race possessing "natural" magic that enables them to "disappear quietly and quickly when large stupid folk like you and me come blundering along" (*Hobbit*, p. 16), is not such an unlikely choice after all as key member of the quest company, as Gandalf well knew.

In the *Departure* segment of the tale we easily identify the elements of call to adventure, refusal of the call and subsequent acceptance, supernatural aid, and crossing the first threshold (corresponding to Vladimir Propp's functions of initial situation, negative and then positive reactions of the hero to persuasion, donor and magical agents, and dispatch of the hero from home). In this preliminary working of the mythic-quest pattern, Tolkien designates the frame of the tale as an "adventure" rather than a "quest," indicative of his still embryonic vision of the events of the Third Age. Yet the simple tale already possesses the mythic structure necessary for the difficult task of mythmaking (Tolkien's term for it is *subcreation*) as the subtitle of the book suggests: "There and Back Again."

The initial situation (α) is located in the land called Hobbiton, where the reader is introduced to a single hobbit whose domestic well-being is about to be interrupted by a subtly veiled interdiction and prophecy (γ).[3] The initial iteration of the call to adventure comes from Gandalf as he interrupts the hobbit's morning smoke in the sun: "I am looking for someone to share in an adventure that I am arranging, and it's very difficult to find anyone." Bilbo's refusal of the call is worded with all the finality he can manage, "We don't want any adventures here, thank you!" Yet the subconscious acceptance of the call is there already, evident in Bilbo's excitement over the identity of the stranger and his notorious feats of magic. In answer to this unspoken receptivity, Gandalf makes the pronouncement that sets Bilbo on the road of the quest, "In fact I will go so far as to send you on this adventure," to which he adds a talisman insuring Bilbo's function as the seeker. With his wizard's staff Gandalf scratches a mysterious rune on the hobbit's tightly closed door. Bilbo's hurried invitation to tea the next day, although intended to get rid of the wizard momentarily, is yet another unconscious acceptance. Bilbo's actual overt response to the call is brought about by the persuasion of a magical agent: Thorin plays upon the golden harp of the dwarves and "Bilbo forgot everything else, and was swept away into dark lands under strange moons, far over The Water and very far from his hobbit-hole under The Hill" (p. 26).

A final observation on this point supplies another instance of the way in which the structural and folkloristic elements at work in this simple tale are carried over into the larger work of the trilogy; the hero must make an official statement of acceptance of the quest (in Propp, this is the beginning of the complication, the conjunctive moment containing the form of the hero's consent, and followed by the form of his dispatch in which the details of the quest are made known to him, including the phenomena to accompany him in the form of magical aids or equipment for the journey). In return for the official assent from the chosen hero, a donor, in this case Gandalf (a function trebled in the figures of Elrond and Beorn; trebling is an important structural device common to mythology and folklore), will bestow upon the hero aids either of a tangible or intangible nature. Bilbo's words "Tell me what you want done, and I will try it" serve as paradigm for the words Frodo is to speak on a fateful night in late October many years in the future.

Both receive magical aids, in Bilbo's case the map of Thror and his silver key to the secret back entrance into the Lonely Mountain. Also in return for the agreement to undertake the task, the hero is instructed in the nature of the quest, what the object sought for may be, and specifically what conduct is expected of the hero. Gandalf and Thorin explain to the overexcited hobbit, in persuasive terms that lure him, frighten him, and finally shame him into wanting to accompany the troupe of dwarves, that the dwarves are on a quest to regain their lost kingdom and treasure in the once-great dwarf city under the Lonely Mountain, now occupied by a "wicked worm," Smaug the Terrible. The expedition is badly in need, Gandalf has assured the dwarves, of a first-class burglar who will know how to extricate the treasure from the claws of the dragon, once he has also figured out how to slip into the ruins of the dwarf kingdom under the mountain.

Thus far we have the initial situation and preparatory section revealed in structural terms of the folkloristic functions. This analysis began with the situation of Bilbo enjoying his prosperity, safe and secure in Hobbiton before the "nasty adventure" presented itself on his doorstep. As Propp explains, "... the initial situation often presents a picture of unusual, sometimes emphasized, prosperity, often in quite vivid, beautiful forms. This prosperity serves as a contrasting background for the ensuing misfortune."[4] We have learned that the only function obligatory to the folkloristic-mythic structure is the function (A) Villainy or (a) Lack; in *The Hobbit* the first function is (a^2) Lack of Wondrous Objects, for the dwarves have a great lack in that they are deprived of kingdom and treasure. This function also serves as motivation for the journey of the hero and master burglar; he is promised his share of the wealth, which he may choose himself. Following the explanation of the lack, the connective incident appears in the form of dispatch and lament (B^4): the dwarves' lay of their lost treasure enchants Bilbo momentarily and causes him to agree to join their cause. Immediately following is the sequence (*DEF*): the donor (Gandalf) presents the company with the map and key, the hero accepts these aids, and the magical agents are transferred from the donor to the head of the expedition, in this case Thorin, although it is the burglar's job to find out how to use them. The final function of this preparatory section is (G^4) Transference or Guidance to a Designated Place, in which the route to the Lonely Mountain is shown to Bilbo and the dwarves. From this point begins the first "move" or series of functions clustered around an act of villainy; each new (*A*) or (*a*) creates a new move, which accounts not only for the seemingly complicated tangle of events in *LOTR*, but as well for its artistically striking balance and symmetry in the simultaneous handling of the various plot lines.

A more modest version of this series occurs in *The Hobbit*, which does not contain the complex juxtaposition of moves traceable in *LOTR*. Fairly simple examples of repetition in moves occur here, which is to say that each act of villainy provides a parallel or paradigm for those that follow, emphasizing the height of the final villainy to which the tale ultimately ascends. Repetition on a more minute level has already occurred in the preparatory section, through the varied entrance of the agents of the donor, the dwarves. This same process will be repeated in the section dealing with Beorn the Skin-changer. They appear on Bilbo's doorstep by degrees, singly or in pairs, but always in increasing permutations of the first entrance: first appears Dwalin; then in like manner Balin; then a pair (" 'Kili at your service!' said the one. 'And Fili!' added the other."); followed by threes, Bifur, Bofur, and Bombur; and by fives, Dori, Nori, Ori, Oin, and Gloin—the names provide the clue to this snowballing effect.

The next step in this first division of *Departure* consists of the first "move" in the mythic structure: crossing the first threshold leads the troupe, on the first leg of the journey, into a confrontation with villainy in the person of several trolls. This encounter will serve as prelude to the more serious types of villainy the company must face further along the road of the quest. Here the villainy is of type (A^1), Threat of Cannibalism. Having trapped all the dwarves in nasty-smelling sacks, the trolls cannot decide "whether they should roast them slowly, or mince them fine and boil them, or just sit on them one by one and squash them into jelly" (p. 50). This dispute proves to be their downfall, for Gandalf, hidden in the bushes, keeps the row smoking until the trolls are trapped by the first rays of the sun and turned to stone. An important connective element should be recognized here in that the villainy of the trolls works toward their own destruction instead of finishing off their victims. Villainy defeats its own purposes often enough through its very nature as evil. W. H. Auden raised this point in his essay on the oppositions in *LOTR* when he considered the fact that Sauron was defeated by himself as much as by his adversaries:

> A good person always enjoys one advantage over an evil person, namely, that, while a good person can imagine what it would be like to be evil, an evil person cannot imagine what it would be like to be good. Elrond, Gandalf, Galadriel, Aragorn are able to imagine themselves as Sauron and can therefore resist the temptation to use the Ring themselves, but Sauron cannot imagine that anyone who knows what the Ring can accomplish, his own destruction among other things, will refrain from using it, let alone try to destroy it.[5]

One finds this concept repeated time and again, both as motivational elements and as connectives. A further step in the structural development has occurred here, a fine example of the way in which Tolkien causes the narrative to fold back upon itself, a frequent device in the narrative sequence. A particular transformation has been applied to the function (A), defined by Propp as *assimilation;* that is, two separate functions assume the same morphological meaning, and thus the Villainy (A) also becomes (D) the Donor and (F) Acquisition of a Magical Agent. More precisely, this functional variation insures that the villainy of the trolls, which caused them to be turned to stone, allows the company to discover their cave unmolested and to help themselves to the magical blades hoarded there: the villains have become donors of magical agents; (A^1) is assimilated to (D^3) Conflict with Hostile Donor and (F^1) Discovery of Magical Agent. A final observation at this stage of the linear sequence concerns the connective element already mentioned. As stated before, Gandalf fulfills the function of helper or supernatural aid, and in that role he becomes the connective agent between moves. He shows up at the moment of crisis to save the beleaguered company from Tom, Bert, and William, thus providing the transition from this first villainy to the crossing of the first threshold beyond the well-secured valley of Rivendell.

Reaching the valley of the elves, the company has crossed out of the "lands we know," to use Lord Dunsany's term, and stops at the Last Homely House on the very edge of the Wild, the dwelling of Elrond Half-elven. Once they leave the valley, they will be setting out on the second part of the quest, the *Initiation* or Road of Trials, or in Propp's terms, the Complication, containing seven related moves. Let us very briefly examine these moves of the *Initiation* for folkloristic structure and content. The first villainy that occurs is the capture of the company by goblins in the Misty Mountains. An important connective incident is the escape of Gandalf in the confusion. It has been noted that Gandalf seems to appear out of nowhere in the nick of time to rescue his friends. The reason behind these sudden appearances is quite clear if we use the morphological analysis. Gandalf fulfills the function (B) or Mediation, the connective incident. He provides the bridge from one move to the next. This same technique is employed with greater facility in *LOTR*, not only in the person of Gandalf but by Aragorn as well. As noted, then, Gandalf reappears in the midst of the goblins in time to save his friends and lop off the head of the Great Goblin: "Suddenly a sword flashed in its own light. Bilbo saw it go right through the Great Goblin as he stood dumbfounded in the middle of his rage. He fell dead, and the goblin soldiers fled before the sword shrieking into the darkness" (p. 72). We have in this first move the sequence (A^2) The Attempt to Murder employing a complication of the type (H-I), Battle With and Defeat of the Villian. The mediation is accomplished, as we said, by the timely return of Gandalf.

The second move is of the same basic sequence (AHI), with

the shift from force to a contest of wits (H^2). We are referring to Bilbo's encounter with Gollum and their riddle game in which Bilbo escapes by cleverness rather than battle, (I^2) Superiority in Contest. One should note here that the connective incident occurs in the form of an inverted villainy, that is, Bilbo finds Gollum's magical ring, (A^3) Seizure of a Magical Agent or Helper, followed by (F negative) in which the agent is not transferred to the original owner. The element of finding a magical agent has undergone repetition (recall that the elvish blades having magical power against goblins were found in the troll cave), this time with implications far surpassing the first instance. In fact, we may plumb the motivations even deeper on this point by determining that the function of the connective is really (F^2) The Agent Appears of Its Own Accord; that is, the Ring allows itself to be found by the hobbit, seemingly choosing to pass out of the hands of Gollum. This is the most pivotal event of the Middle-earth mythology, for it not only emphasizes the immanence of power in the natural objects of Middle-earth (the powers inherent in the elves and Sauron flowed into the Ring at its making) but provides the fundamental motivating force for this first tale and the larger one to come. The possession of the Ring gives to the hero the attribute of invisibility, which in the present tale undergoes repetition by appearing in each of the succeeding moves as the means of rescue: from the spiders, the wood-elves, Smaug the dragon, and in the battle of the Three Armies from the dwarves. A final observation of this move discloses that the death of the Great Goblin also becomes a connective function in that it provides the motivation for several of the moves that follow, in particular the concluding move.

The Goblin's demise is motivation for the pursuit by the lesser goblins and wild wargs, ending in the entrapment of the company in trees ringing the foothills of the Misty Mountains. Here a paired set of functions follows the villainy (A^2) Threat of Murder; the functions (H-I) mentioned before appear with the elements (Pr^1) Pursuit of the Hero in an attempt to destroy him and (Rs^1) Rescue by Air, when the eagles drawn by the yammering and yelping swooped down upon the goblins and "the dark rush of their beating wings smote them to the floor or drove them far away; their talons tore at goblin faces" (p. 110). The connective incident here is (G^1) Transference of Hero to Designated Place, in this case by air, when the eagles deposit the adventurers near the cabin of Beorn, the donor of this same move. The donor follows the form of (D^2) Greeting and Interrogation, to confer his aid, also accompanied by repetition of auxiliary elements; the dwarves are introduced to him in the same manner in which Bilbo encountered them, by degrees and in pairs or name groups, while Gandalf keeps the intimidating shapeshifter's attention distracted with the tale of their ordeal in reaching his settlement (B^2, Announcement of Misfortune): "Mr. Baggins saw then how clever Gandalf had been. The interruptions had really made Beorn more interested in the story, and the story had kept him from sending the dwarves off at once like suspicious beggars. . . . Now he had got fifteen strangers sitting on his porch!" (p. 126).

The connecting functions for the next move occur in the form of (a^1) Lack of a Helper and (A^4) Casting a Spell. The new villainy of the confrontation with the spiders in the forest of Mirkwood is a result of the fact that Gandalf decides to leave the troupe on their own just as they enter the forest, and once in the forest they break his interdiction to stay on the path and avoid the enchantment of the wood-elves. The sequence once again follows the pattern of battle with and victory over the villains, Bilbo again making use of the invisibility granted by the power of the Ring. His cleverness again becomes evident as he leads the spiders off on a wild chase to rescue his friends; from now on the dwarves expect him to figure out what to do as a matter of course; his stature as hero has begun to develop noticeably. This same gradual development of heroic qualities can also be recognized in the second Ringbearer, Frodo.

The next move includes their capture by the wood-elves, (A^5) Capture and Imprisonment, and the rescue performed as before by Bilbo with the aid of the magic Ring. The type of complication involved here, however, is not (H-I) but rather (M-N) a Difficult Task and its Solution, the task being to discover a method for releasing the dwarves from their elvish prison. This sequence is repeated within the same move when the company find themselves high on the Lonely Mountain trying to uncover the secret entrance mentioned by the map and opened only by the silver key. Again, Bilbo solves the riddle, just in time to make use of the key as "a red ray of the sun escaped like a finger through a rent in the cloud" exposing in a pinpoint of light the long-sought keyhole.

As on previous occasions in which Bilbo has gone prowling about in the dark tunnels under mountains, he provides the connective motivation for the next move by a function of reversed villainy, (A^6) Plundering or Theft; that is, Bilbo lifts a golden cup from under the steaming nose of the great red-gold dragon. This is an excellent example of the growth of heroism in Bilbo, accentuated by Smaug's dream of "a warrior, altogether insignificant in size but provided with a bitter sword and a great courage" troubling his ancient sleep. The actual villainy of this move, however, is the assault of Smaug upon the men of Laketown at the bottom of the foothills, where once again the functions are (H-I). As before, evil engenders its own downfall, for Smaug is killed by the black-shafted arrow of Bard, which pierces the only unprotected spot in the diamond waistcoat of the worm. The dragon's pride in the jewels encrusted on his breast from lying on the hoard for centuries causes him to forget the bare spot over his heart.

As the threads of the narrative pull together, the connectives and motivational functions become more complex, particularly in the crucial move of the *Initiation*, bringing about the climax of the quest. Both functions (a^2) Threat of Murder and (A^7) Declaration of War are assimilated into the beginning of this next move; a lack (Thorin cannot find the Arkenstone because it has been stolen by his own burglar, Tolkien's masterful touch of irony), caused once again by the inverted villainy of the hero perpetrating a theft of a wondrous object, is assimilated with the villainy of a declaration of hostilities. The dwarves are pitted against the elves and men who come to claim part of the treasure as their due for killing the frightful guardian of the hoard. Through the effects of repetition, the war of greed mushrooms into a war of survival when the forces of the mountain goblins pour down upon the besiegers at the same moment as the dwarvish reinforcements of Dain from the Iron Hills reach the site of battle. Aid reappears in the form of the eagles and Beorn. Other connective incidents operative here are the unexpected return of Gandalf among the troops from Laketown and his performance of the function (*F neg*) in refusing to return the Arkenstone to Thorin. The death of Thorin in battle is the final statement of the self-destructive attribute of evil, for once the dwarvish greed had advanced in Thorin to the point that he was willing to kill and declare war because of it, his hours were numbered.

The victory of the forces of good over the goblins and wargs brings the tale to the *Return*, in which Bilbo and company, laden with gifts from the treasure pile (W^1, Gain of Wealth at Denouement), return to the ordinary daylight world of the "lands we know." This comprises the final move, in which the villainy is of a homely kind, appropriate to its location in Hobbition: Bilbo's relatives have confiscated his lovely hobbit hole because his year's absence has convinced them he is dead. The function (*Q*) Recognition of Hero brings about the sequence (H-I^3) Expulsion of the Villain, as he puts an end to the auction being carried out in his front yard. In the three-part scheme of the hero quest, the returning wanderer often finds readmission to society a difficult matter, even though he may have brought back a wonderful boon to the people or profitted himself by the venture. As the reader can discern, the sedentary hobbits were now wary of the prodigal: "he was in fact held by all the hobbits of the neighbourhood to be 'queer' "; yet to his credit "he remained an elf-friend, and had the honour of dwarves, wizards, and all such folk as ever passed that way."

The forces of opposition and the pull toward mediation or resolution have been demonstrated on the structural level of the linear sequence, with some slight indication of the same operations at work in the content and mythic motifs that make up the substance of the tale. We find instances of opposition in the delineation of character as well as action. J. S. Ryan's analysis of Tolkien's use of the "literary folk memory" gives the following example: against the winged manifestation of "the dragon symbol as a means of showing opposing evil in the world" Tolkien sets the eagles "as supreme forces of good which appear at decisive moments in both the great battle sequences [of *The Hobbit* and *LOTR*]."[6] Or on a broader level, the use of repetition is also a method for injecting irony into the tale as well as emphasis. The hero returns from peril as the bringer of the grail to humanity. Bilbo the burglar has freed the Lake people from Smaug's tyranny of fear, reestablished Bard as lord in the ruined city of Dale, and brought into the community of Hobbiton fabulous wealth, which he gives away, as well as having helped reinstate the dwarves once more in their old halls under the Lonely Mountain. Yet he also bears into Hobbiton the One Ring, causing the sleepy region of nonadventurous folk to become the seat of the most dread evil and power imaginable, but a power that will also free the world of Middle-earth from the clutches of Sauron once the Ring is destroyed. Thus the local boon for Hobbiton will develop into the universal boon for the wide world. As Lévi-Strauss predicted, there is both logic and continuity in even the most seemingly simple mythic tale. Having demonstrated with *The Hobbit* the type of analysis employed in this book, we move now into the major concern of this study, the composition of *The Lord of the Rings*.

CHAPTER 3

Subcreation and
the Three Heroes

AN IMPORTANT CONCEPT CONSIDERED EARLIER in this book, that "a totally new type of non-theological revelation, of great scope, great depth, and infinite variety [the mythmaking potential of the artist], has become the actual spiritual guide and structuring force of the civilization,"[1] turns up in Tolkien's essay on the fairy story, illuminating that role yet another degree. As indicated previously, if the artist is to create a truly relevant new mythological construct for twentieth-century minds, he must offer them vital, fresh associations filled with the potential for inspiration. Clearly what Joseph Campbell means by "creative mythology" and what Professor Tolkien has in mind when he described the link between imagination and its resultant art of subcreation are one and same. Quoting from Campbell on this subject, "the individual . . . seeks to communicate through signs; and if his realization has been of a certain depth and import, his communication will have the value and force of living myth—for those, that is to say, who receive and respond to it of themselves, with recognition, uncoerced."[2] One finds the same idea iterated in Tolkien's essay:

> Creative fantasy, because it is mainly trying to do something else (make something new), may open your hoard and let all the locked things fly away like cage-birds. The gems all turn into flowers or flames, and you will be warned that all you had (or knew) was dangerous and potent, not really effectively chained, free and wild; no more yours than they were you.[3]

The role of the artist, then, for Tolkien is to undertake genuine subcreation rather than generate mere "representations or symbolic interpretation of the beauties and terrors of the world." If the artist has listened with his inner ear to the truth within himself, the myth he creates will reflect it. William Ready's observations on the nature of tale telling elucidate the manner in which Tolkien's work meets this requirement: "There is one real purpose in Story; to reveal a truth by a tale, a tale that can be read for itself with enjoyment and yet where, upon reflection—which may or may not come—Truth enters in, often as unwelcome and forbidding as a creed."[4] Transmitted through the properly receptive medium of the true mythmaker, the mythic impulse does not lie.

Backtracking to a more verifiable sphere of evidence, yet in the mainstream of what we have just said, this subcreation exhibits a predictable folkloristic structure quite as much in *LOTR* as we saw in *The Hobbit*, and certainly on a grander scale. As Claude Lévi-Strauss puts it, "if there is a meaning to be found in mythology, this cannot reside in the isolated elements which enter into the composition of a myth, but only in the way those elements are combined. . . . the true constituent units of a myth are not the isolated relations but *bundles of such relations* . . . combined so as to produce a meaning."[5] Having taken one step forward and two steps backward, let us move directly to a consideration of these elements in the first of the plot lines pursuing the hero quest in *LOTR*.

Consider first the various ways in which the *Departure* stage is woven into the role Gandalf plays in the cataclysmic events of the Third Age of Middle-earth. As the analysis unfolds, the reader will be tracing the wizard's development as supernatural helper, warrior, and sage, three separate manifestations of the hero character found in mythology. Gandalf's call to adventure comes before the beginning of the *Fellowship of the Ring*.[6] He hints of this to Frodo in his attempt to impress upon the hobbit the nature of the seemingly innocent gold trinket willed to him by his aged uncle Bilbo; a test by fire will reveal whether it is the One Ring, a knowledge Gandalf must have: "I have come back from dark journeys and long search to make that final test" (Book I, p. 88). By implication we know that Gandalf has already accepted the call without hesitation; he must now convey that urgency to an extremely hesitant hobbit by revealing that "great perils" lie before the wizard. As the nature of Gandalf's call becomes unveiled, we realize that his quest is to be carried out on the highest level of the structure (universal) although the three protagonists all share in the same quest on their own individual levels. Frodo observes: "But this business of ours will be his [Gandalf's] greatest task."

Gandalf explains where the crossing of the first threshold should occur, a direction that applies to all three heroes, Frodo and Aragorn included. "If you want my advice," he tells Frodo, "make for Rivendell. That journey should not prove too perilous, though the Road is less easy than it was [when Bilbo traversed it heading for Rivendell], and it will grow worse as the year fails." The hero often encounters difficulty in crossing the first threshold into the lands of adventure and peril; for example, only supernatural aid coming in the final minutes of flight for the borders of Rivendell saves the heroes from the Nazgul, agents of the Enemy. At the very moment when the Nazgul leader pushes his horse into the stream separating him from the stricken Frodo, the magic immanent in nature comes to the rescue: the River awakens:

> At that moment there came a roar and a rushing: a noise of loud waters rolling many stones. Dimly Frodo saw the river below him rise, and down along its course there came a plumed cavalry of waves. White flames seemed to Frodo to flicker on their crests and he half fancied that he saw amid the water white riders upon white horses with frothing manes. The three Riders that were still in the midst of the Ford were overwhelmed: they disappeared, buried suddenly under angry foam. Those that were behind drew back in dismay. (I, p. 286)

This is the magic of which Tolkien has spoken, magic that flows naturally from the heart of Faerie and not a magician's box of tricks. Yet safely in Rivendell, the company may not rest too easily, for as Gandalf warns them, ". . . we have reached Rivendell, but the Ring is not yet at rest." He is wary, for wizard though he is, he has required several instances of supernatural aid to bring him to the first threshold of Rivendell. For instance,

trapped in the tower of Saruman, he was rescued by his friend
from *The Hobbit*, Gwaihir the eagle, and received swift passage
to the enchanted valley on the back of Shadowfax, king of horses
possessing such speed and power as no ordinary horse can
boast; such beasts of nature are filled with natural magic, for no
rider whom Shadowfax consents to bear can fall from his back
although he allows no saddle or bridle to touch him. Here in
Rivendell plans for the second stage of the quest, the Road of
Trials in the *Initiation*, must be made and the quest itself deter-
mined, a grave decision, voiced by Gandalf: "Here we all are,
and here is the Ring. But we have not yet come any nearer to our
purpose. What shall we do with it?" (I, p. 347).

Frodo's acknowledgement of the call to adventure and his
final acceptance of its burden is the more immediate subject of
the opening pages of the *Fellowship*, whereas Gandalf's call is
presented mainly through implication. It is important that
Frodo's adventure actually begins on the day he comes of age;
this is also Bilbo's birthday, and the celebration of their dual
party by Gandalf, hobbits, and dwarves begins the pre-
liminaries of the call, which does not come directly until a
number of years later. The air of mystery generated by these
preparations for the grand birthday party sets the atmosphere
for the adventure no one suspects is coming. Frodo is not yet ripe
for the hero's role, for instead Bilbo responds to the call for the
second time in his life. But this time the call reaches beyond
Bilbo to Frodo and others, as Bilbo's prophetic walking song
indicates:

> Now far ahead the Road has gone,
> And I must follow, if I can,
> Pursuing it with eager feet,
> Until it joins some larger way
> Where many paths and errands meet.
> And whither then: I cannot say. (I, p. 62)

Frodo's call begins indirectly with his ownership of the Ring
(" 'The ring!' exclaimed Frodo. 'Has he left me that? I wonder
why,' "), but he does not hear the distant summons at this point.
The call works subtly in Frodo, as he begins to feel a growing
restlessness and desire to follow Bilbo to Rivendell, where the

old hobbit had gone to pass the remainder of his days. Frodo's fiftieth birthday has ominous overtones; it was that age at which "adventure had suddenly befallen Bilbo. Frodo began to feel restless, and the old paths seemed too well-trodden." Finally, Gandalf himself comes to give the call to Frodo directly and invest him with the quest. He tries to convince Frodo that Bilbo was meant to find the Ring, "in which case you were also *meant* to have it," he tells Frodo. " 'And now,' said the wizard, turning back to Frodo, 'the decision lies with you. . . . Have you decided what to do?' " The call cannot have a plainer statement.

Frodo's crossing of the first threshold proves as difficult as Gandalf's, for he is pursued by the agents of the villain to the very borders of Rivendell, as we have seen. In addition to eluding the terror of the horsemen, Frodo and his three companion hobbits must cross through the Old Forest in which they lose their way, traversing the valley of the Withywindle harboring such obstacles as Old Man Willow and the barrow wights. At Bree an attempt is made on Frodo's life, and farther down the road he and his company must turn to fight the Nazgul face to face, a confrontation culminating in the flight to the ford of the river.

The third hero, Aragorn, like Frodo, receives the call from Gandalf. The wizard first approaches Aragorn as a fellow traveler, asking his aid in searching for the creature Gollum, who once owned the Ring as we have learned from *The Hobbit,* and this enlistment sets Aragorn upon the path of the ultimate quest. Aragorn's formal statement that he has accepted the call is voiced when he joins Frodo's company in the inn at Bree against their desires. In spite of their protestations, he says, "just this: you must take me along with you, until I wish to leave you." He makes it clear to the hobbits that the "secret" they are carrying out of the Shire concerns himself and his friends as well as Gandalf and the hobbits; thus the quest is expanded threefold, as we have indicated. From this point, Aragorn's crossing of the first threshold coincides with that of Frodo, including the stand taken upon Weathertop and the flight to the ford at Rivendell.

Having charted the three hero lines as they fit into the *Departure* pattern of the mythic quest, we can determine the individual component parts in the folkloristic structure within this larger framework, coming finally, through Lévi-Strauss, to the arrangement of the narrative in three-dimensional form. Commonly the functions of the myth appear in pairs or triplets, such as *ABC* (villainy, mediation, counteraction), *DEF* (donor, hero's response, magical agent), *H-I* (battle with villain, hero's victory), *MN* (difficult task, solution), *PrRs* (pursuit, rescue). Again, this is the effect of repetition and trebling. Propp also discovered that there were four combinations of elements in the complication that are basic to folklore structures: (*H-I*), (*MN*), both, or neither, with variation produced by inversions, assimilations, and insertions of other functions between pairs. One should keep in mind as well that each separate "move" centers around its own hero, from the act of villainy or lack to the final rescue or arrival at a desired state. In the immediately preceding analysis of the first part of *LOTR*, *Departure* corresponds to the first move of Propp's schema and also follows precisely the seven divisions into which the functions of the myth cohere as a complete narrative, which were enumerated in chapter 1. In addition, Tolkien's framework is further complicated by assimilation of moves within moves, trebling, repetition, and use of parallel elements.

The use of the folkloristic techniques just mentioned leads one at first to conclude that the structure of the trilogy is exhaustingly complex. However, the exciting paradoxical discovery made possible through the morphological analysis is the beautiful simplicity of the tale of the Ring as a whole. We have said that in mythic structure, each new villainy constitutes a separate move or sequence of functions. At first observation the trilogy seems to be made up of an endless number of villainies, complicating the structure manyfold. A return to the morphological analysis reveals, contrarily, that this is a case of not seeing the forest for the trees. After carefully examining the types of structures produced by the folkloristic mind in the tales he covered, Vladimir Propp discovered that the sequence most basic to the mythic imagination was that of two moves, invariably in the same ordering—first battle with the enemy and then solution of a difficult task:

If a tale consists of two moves, then moves containing a fight always precede those involving tasks. Hence we conclude that a move with H-I is a typical first move, and a move with difficult tasks is a typical second or repeated move. . . . What conclusions does this scheme present? In the first place, it affirms our general thesis regarding the total uniformity in the construction of fairy tales. . . . As has already been indicated, this conclusion appeared quite unexpectedly. It was an unexpected one for the author of this work as well. This phenomenon is so unusual and strange that one somehow feels a desire to dwell upon it, prior to going on to more particular, formal conclusions. . . . Yet one still feels inclined to pose this question: if all fairy tales are so similar in form, does this not mean that they all originate from a single source? . . . The single source may also be a psychological one.[7]

Thus, regarding the entire trilogy, we realize it is indeed only two moves: (1) fight with the villain or his agents and victory (*H-I*), which is the *Departure* section under consideration presently; and (2) difficult task and solution (*MN*), the *Initiation* section to be discussed in part two of this book. Admittedly this second move is greatly expanded by the method of assimilation on a grand scale, containing moves of smaller sequences within the larger one, to allow the development of each of the three heroes of the tale; yet one cannot fail to see that even this complex modern myth in its three-book length fits the basic two-move structure Propp discovered in his study of Russian fairy tales.

With this in mind, let us return to our analysis of the functions and details of structure in the first move of *LOTR*, following Propp's seven divisions of functions.

Division I. The Initial Situation

We are given the "temporal-spatial determination" and the family composition or situation of Bilbo and his adopted heir Frodo Baggins in Hobbiton. Also presented here is their well-being before the complication.

Division II. The Preparatory Section

Absentation of the elders occurs when Bilbo disappears at his birthday party, held also in honor of Frodo. Gandalf first delivers an interdiction by cautioning Frodo to avoid using the Ring, and on his return years later issues a command in the form of the "call" as we termed it earlier, insisting that Frodo must leave Hobbiton. The first appearance of the agents of the villain and their reconnaissance is accomplished through the Black Riders who suddenly sweep through Hobbiton, inquiring for "Mr. Baggins of Bag End."

Division III. The Complication

Here the inversion transformation has been applied to the functions (ABC ↑) in that the departure or dispatch of the hero from home occurs first, although the threat of villainy from the Black Riders is the motivating force for departure. The actual villainy (A^2 Threat of Murder) occurs in the form of pursuit by the Riders, which is interrupted by the approach of Gildor and some High Elves (B^3 Entrance of Intermediaries), functioning here as the conjunctive element. Mediation is accomplished by the presence of the elves warding off the agents of the enemy. The connective incident occurs when the intermediary, Gildor, recognizes the presence of the hero, for Frodo speaks to him in Elvish. " 'Be careful, friends!" cried Gildor laughing. 'Speak no secrets! Here is a scholar in the Ancient Tongue. Bilbo was a good master. Hail, Elf-friend!' he said, bowing to Frodo" (I, p. 119). This is also the function (Q), Recognition of the Hero, which is trebled by the subsequent recognitions of the other two heroes, Aragorn and Gandalf.

The appearance of Gildor introduces another element, the entrance of helpers, that will be followed from here on in addition to the functions of the characters. There are three species of helper according to our morphology: (1) the *universal helper* who may assist the hero in many ways, usually a human or similar creature; (2) a *partial helper* who may serve in a limited capacity in more than one instance in the plot, usually an animal or character of only a few appearances; and (3) the *specific helper*, usually an object with magical properties that plays a part in only one event or serves the hero in only one capacity. The entry of a live helper is most often a connective incident, for he either conveys information or advice or gets information from the hero that becomes a motivating element further on in the tale. Gildor serves this function in the last section of this first move. Here he is a universal helper, as are Frodo's hobbit companions, Sam, Merry, and Pippin. The pursuit is continued, and the hobbits' arrival at Farmer Maggot's house serves as another connective, with Maggot as a partial helper in that he provides the hobbits with safe passage over the bridge into Buckland, thereby thwarting the Black Riders from seizing their prey on his lands. The close pursuit by the agents of Sauron has caused the hobbits to abandon their plan for an unobtrusive stay in Buckland, seeking cover instead in the Old Forest, (*C*, Counteraction).

Division IV. Donors

The journey to the home of the donors (Tom Bombadil and Goldberry) is brought about by the enchantment thrown over the hobbits in the ancient wood and the valley of the Withywindle. The forest itself determines their course in spite of the way they intended to take through it: "Each time they clambered out, the trees seemed deeper and darker; and always to the left and upwards it was most difficult to find a way, and they were forced to the right and downwards," down into the enchanted valley of the River Withywindle. What appears to be a new villainy at this point (Old Man Willow traps Merry in a crack in his trunk) is actually a connective incident providing the motivation for the inclusion of the first donor into the tale.

There is one point that will prove important time and again to the development of the tale. The connective and motivational incidents are most often functions carried out by that magical power immanent in nature discussed earlier: the aura of Faerie itself, a force one must deal with in the lands beyond those we know. This elemental mythic ingredient acknowledged by Tolkien points up the inadequacy of interpretations that insist it is the Christian God who drives Frodo to be crucified upon Mount Doom. Rather, in broader mythic terms, it is the immanent magic of the natural world of Middle-earth, not heaven, that propels the tale to its completion. Tolkien's own statements on this subject are enlightening:

> Andrew Lang said, and is by some still commended for saying, that mythology and religion (in the strict sense of that word) are two distinct things that have become inextricably entangled, though mythology is in itself almost devoid of religious significance. . . . Even fairy-stories as a whole have three faces: the Mystical towards the Supernatural; the Magical towards Nature; and the Mirror of scorn and pity towards Man. The essential face of Faerie is the middle one, the Magical.[8]

Frodo's call for help brings Tom Bombadil, the nature deity par excellence, who fulfills an assimilated function here, (Rs^2) Rescue by Intervention of Helpers and (K^1) Breaking of a Spell. Tom and Goldberry are a male and female pair of universal helpers preparing the reader for a greater such pair whose magic comes from cosmic sources of stars and moonlight rather than vegetal, seasonal sources, that is, Celeborn and Galadriel. We are apprised of the donor's dwelling, physical appearance, and his hospitality to the hero, but most important, of his subtle test of the hero. The test takes place through the function (T^3), Transformation through Enchantment, in which Frodo spitefully puts on the Ring to awe Bombadil; the reader will recall that Tom has shown so little regard for the Ring that he even has the nerve to put it on and fail to disappear. As Frodo tries to slip out the door, Tom cries, "Hey! Come Frodo, there! Where be you a-going? Old Tom Bombadil's not as blind as that yet. Take off your golden ring! Your hand's more fair without it. Come back! Leave your game and sit down beside me! We must talk a while more, and think about the morning. Tom must teach the right road, and keep your feet from wandering" (I, p. 185). The natural magic of Tom is so ancient that the golden circlet does not affect him, even though elvish power is infused in it.

The donor's advice also takes the form of an interdiction, for this section is preparatory to the next lesser villainy, which is still part of the larger division of encounter with the donor. Thus we have an example of two smaller moves within the first large one, acting as microcosms; twice Tom rescues the hobbits from forces in the borders of his domain. This is a complex knot to unravel, for the adventure with the barrow wights (which results from the breaking of the interdiction "Keep to the green grass. Don't you go a-meddling with old stone or cold Wights or prying in their houses, unless you be strong folk with hearts that never falter!") becomes the means by which the function (*F*), Acquisition of a Magical Agent or specific helper, is accomplished. When Frodo recites the charm taught him by Tom (*B*¹, Call for Help) it immediately brings the donor to the rescue, once more breaking a spell. This time Tom rescues the hobbits from a barrow where Frodo has exerted his developing heroic abilities (*H-I* occurs, as Frodo stabs the cold hand of the wight before it can reach him) and piles up the treasures of the barrow in the open sun. From this pile the hobbits equip themselves with bright blades forged in timeless ages past by the legendary men of Westernesse who, Tom tells them, still remain in few numbers, protecting "heedless" folk like themselves. Another important connective function is performed here in the form of a prophecy, a device encountered frequently in the course of the tale:

> The hobbits did not understand his words, but as he spoke they had a vision as it were of a great expanse of years behind them, like a vast shadowy plain over which there strode shapes of Men, tall and grim with bright swords, and last came one with a star on his brow. Then the vision faded, and they were back in the sunlit world. (I, p. 201)

The general sequence for this division is (*DEF*). The major connective function leading into the next division is (*G*) Guidance of the Hero to Designated Place, for Tom is obliged to lead the hobbits the rest of the way to the main road leading into Bree.

Division V. Entry of Major Helper to End of First Move

Division V continues the villainy (pursuit by agents of

enemy) begun in Division III, the complication. Several connective elements here serve to bring the tale back into the area of the first basic function (A^2). The first element is an attribute of the characters—both Frodo and Aragorn have assumed disguises at Bree. The functions (T) and (Q) act as motivations for the major conjunctive moment (B^3), the entry of the universal helper Strider into the tale through his acceptance into Frodo's band. The Ring reveals itself for the second time, causing Frodo to disappear before the eyes of the startled occupants of the inn. Thus the Ringbearer is made known to Aragorn through the function (Q) in which his transformation into invisibility is the identifying factor. A final motivational element, Gandalf's letter, by which they may test the identity of Strider, completes the acceptance of Strider into the company.

An interesting assimilation occurs at this point, providing further motivation for the villainy. With the hobbits safely quartered at Bree, Tolkien takes us back to Buckland in time to witness the attack of the agents of Mordor upon the house in which Frodo was supposedly living. Once they realize they have missed him, the pursuit is intensified, culminating in the direct confrontation at Weathertop. To prepare for this, Tolkien has assimilated the villainy just mentioned with a further villainy (also A^2), in which the cushions made up to look like sleeping hobbits are knifed to shreds in the inn. It becomes clear that these apparent villainies are really connectives preparing us for the actual villainy in which Frodo is wounded by the blade from Mordor. The concurrent theft of their ponies on the night the cushions are slashed is a motivational element by which a partial helper is added to the company. They are forced to buy an old nag, which surprisingly serves them well in the days to come. Once the pursuit is resumed, the functions remaining at the end of the first move occur as follows:

1. Second appearance of the agents of the villain (the Ringwraiths surround the company on the bare summit of Weathertop hill)

2. Third appearance or trebling of the object of the quest (the Ring reveals itself to the Ringwraiths, as well as suddenly allowing its wearer to see them clearly)

3. Struggle with the villain (H^1) as the Black Riders attack

4. Marking of the hero (J^1) in which Frodo is wounded by the blade of the wraith King

5. Victory over the villain (I^1), accomplished as much by Frodo's utterance of the elvish name "Elbereth" as by Strider's firebrands

The final functions of the first move, further pursuit and rescue, are carried through in the following manner. With the healing powers of *athelas* (an herb known to Aragorn, which serves as a specific helper), Frodo is revived enough to be carried on the one horse (partial helper) in their flight to the ford at the borders of Rivendell (G^2). At the first bridge the operative function is (F^1). A magical agent (specific helper) is found in the form of the green gem elfstone, a connective element in that it tells the company the bridge is safe at this point, and they may pass on unmolested. The conjunctive moment before the rescue (B^3, Entrance of Intermediaries) comes in the person of Glorfindel, a High Elf prince (a universal helper), who has kept watch for the travelers because of the message sent him by Gildor that the Ringbearer was making for Rivendell. The end of the first move, the rescue, is brought about by the powers of nature itself, a function previously observed in the episode with Tom Bombadil. Here the Great River rises with its own magic at the instant the evil forces step into its waters, (Rs^2), enabling the company to reach Rivendell safely and the second part of the tale to commence.

PART TWO
INITIATION

CHAPTER 4

Trial, Death, and Transfiguration

THE SUBTLE BEAUTIES OF FORM AND CONTENT referred to in the prologue are given in this part the greatest benefit of Tolkien's creative imagination, skillfully leading the reader along the various lines of the narration. In following this central development of the quest myth, we become increasingly aware of the play of opposition and mediation, of the paradigmatic patterns within the linear structure of the trilogy. In addition, our attention is more specifically directed toward the rituals of human experience as the Fellowship is split up and we follow each of the heroes individually. The human quest for integration and unity, "at-one-ment," awaits each of the heroes at the end of the road.

Crossing the first threshold into Rivendell becomes the paradigm for a greater pattern of separation-reunion to come. Here Frodo and his company are unexpectedly reunited with Gandalf and Bilbo, strengthening their courage and resolve. In this instance the mediating function of reunion is motivational, whereas in the reunion at the end of the quest the purpose is reward. This first mediation is necessary for the development of the hero consciousness in Frodo, Aragorn, and Gandalf, for here each acknowledges his true identity: Gandalf as a wizard of extraordinary, although untested, capabilities; Aragorn as the last heir of the kingship to ancient Numenor; and Frodo as the most essential hero of all, the Ringbearer. Gandalf's unsuspected heroic stature begins to dawn on the hobbits as they note the manner in which he is deferred to at the Council of Elrond where many high and important personages are gathered. In answer to many questions, Elrond explains that "these things it is the part of Gandalf to make clear; and I call upon him last, for it the place of honour, and in all this matter he has been the chief" (I, p. 328). In a demonstration of his authority, Gandalf dares to speak the language of Mordor within the confines of Rivendell by reading the inscription on the deadly Ring: "The change in the wizard's voice was astounding. Suddenly it became menacing, powerful, harsh as stone. A shadow seemed to pass over the high sun, and the porch for a moment grew dark. All trembled, and the Elves stopped their ears" at the sound of the hated words. "Never before has any voice dared to utter words of that tongue in Imladris, Gandalf the Grey," whispers the astonished Elrond, which makes explicit Gandalf's authority, in that he is allowed to get away with the act.

Aragorn, too, unveils his true identity in an impressive manner: Frodo is commanded to hold up the Ring so the eyes of the doubting Boromir may behold "Isildur's Bane." Elrond then points to Strider, its rightful owner by inheritance, saying, "He is Aragorn son of Arathorn, . . . and he is descended through many fathers from Isildur Elendil's son of Minas Ithil. He is the Chief of the Dunedain in the North, and few are now left of that folk" (I, p. 324). But the emergence of Frodo as the Ringbearer is perhaps the most dramatic revelation of all. After debating about what must be done with the Ring, the Council admits that any solution other than "unmaking" the dread object is only another delay. When all the assembly of great folk explain why they may not take possession of the Ring and sit with "downcast eyes," Frodo realizes with dread that he must bear the burden. "At last with an effort he spoke, and wondered to hear his own words, as if some other will was using his small voice."

" 'I will take the Ring,' he said, 'though I do not know the way.' " Here we are struck with Tolkien's power to evoke human poignancy and suffering, that chief imprint of our human experience that Joseph Campbell calls "the raw material of tragedy" and is "in a preliminary sense at least, the sum and effect of all."[1] In Frodo's simple statement the reader instantly understands what is meant by the "grave and constant" quality of life. For Frodo it becomes a prophecy of the ordeal by fire through which he will pass at the end of the road, a transformation described in Campbell's *Primitive Mythology:* "The only true wisdom lives far from mankind, out in the great loneliness, and it can be reached only through suffering. Privation and suffering alone can open the mind of a man to all that is hidden to others."[2]

As Campbell rightly observes in *The Hero with the Thousand Faces*, this phase of the quest dealing with the hero's ordeals and trials along the road to his goal is a favorite topic in literature, providing an author with an excellent chance to display his powers of description and invention to their best advantage. Campbell's catalog of the mythical motifs and devices supporting this phase of the quest-journey contains an observation pertinent to the concept of the immanent power of the natural world: the hero sets foot on the Road of Trials bearing with him the magical devices or charms of his supernatural helper, or "it may be that he here discovers for the first time that there is a benign power everywhere supporting him in his superhuman passage."[3] The reader discovers as he follows the progress of the Ring to its destruction in the Cracks of Mount Doom that this "benign power" provides the motivating and conjunctive elements initiating the accomplishment of the many formidable tasks confronting Frodo and his companions, even to the extent that the very powers of evil work toward this end ("Evil will evil mar" says Theoden).

Of Tolkien's three heroes, Frodo is the first we shall follow along the Road of Trials, as his quest, the destruction of the One Ring, is the most critical to the history of the Third Age as well as to the structure of the trilogy (we will be able to deduce this fact from the morphological analysis of this second move of the tale). This vantage point of Frodo's progress further illuminates the development of the other two heroes, Aragorn and Gandalf. It is important to see the trilogy in this way, for Tolkien consistently reminds his readers that the three heroes and their individual fates are inextricably bound together when he suspends the narrative line of one hero to reveal what is occurring simultaneously to the other members of the Fellowship. For example, Merry's reaction to the sundering of the Fellowship emphasizes the separate quest of each hero: "They have all left me now.

They have all gone to some doom: Gandalf and Pippin to war in
the East; and Sam and Frodo to Mordor; and Strider and
Legolas and Gimli to the Paths of the Dead. But my turn will
come soon enough, I suppose" (III, p. 83). Shortly afterwards
Tolkien draws these divergent threads together when Sam,
lonely in the hopeless wastes of Mordor, faces the west and
wonders what has become of his friends of the Fellowship:

> Out westward in the world it was drawing to noon upon the
> fourteenth day of March in the Shire-reckoning, and even now
> Aragorn was leading the black fleet from Pelargir, and Merry was
> riding with the Rohirrim down the Stonewain Valley, while in
> Minas Tirith flames were rising and Pippin watched the madness
> growing in the eyes of Denethor. Yet amid all their cares and fear
> the thoughts of their friends turned constantly to Frodo and Sam.
> (III, p. 212)

Consequently, we find it next to impossible to talk exclusively
about Frodo, then about Aragorn, and then Gandalf, for often
the progress of one includes another. The Road of Trials is the
same for all three to the point at which Gandalf falls from the
bridge of Khazad-dum into the abyss. For Frodo and Aragorn,
the remaining two heroes, the road is the same until their
separation at the Falls of Rauros, where we can begin to track
them individually.

For Frodo *Initiation* means following the Road of Trials to
the Meeting with the Goddess, Atonement with the Father, and
the resulting Ultimate Boon. To set out on his journey, Frodo is
equipped with supplies, nine companions, and as much lore and
advice as can be gathered. Elrond speaks to Frodo of the road in
these terms: "I can foresee very little of your road; and how your
task is to be achieved I do not know. . . . You will meet many
foes, some open, and some disguised; and you may find friends
upon your way when you least look for it" (I, p. 360). The first
obstacle materializes as a blizzard hurled upon their heads by
the malice of the mountain Caradhras, in which Frodo nearly
freezes to death but for the efforts of the company. With this way
barred to them, they seek passage under the mountain through
the deserted mines of Moria. Here we make note of the change

taking place in Frodo, a foreshadowing of greater changes to come as he grows in his role as Ringbearer, for the wound he received from the blade of Mordor has sharpened his senses so he becomes more aware of "things that could not be seen." The company's loss of Gandalf in the labyrinthine tunnels of Moria constitutes the first disaster attending the Road of Trials. Here Aragorn's role as hero begins to take shape, for now he must become the leader of the journey in the place of Gandalf. Through his guidance the Ringbearer passes these initial obstacles safely, ready for the next stage of the journey.

The meeting with the goddess is visualized in *LOTR* as the company's reception by the High Elves in Lothlorien and in particular the Lady of the enchanted wood, Galadriel, keeper of one of the Three Rings saved by the elves from the corrupting influence of the One Ring. Campbell has this to say about the goddess of the quest myth: ". . . she is the incarnation of the promise of perfection. . . . Time sealed her away, yet she is dwelling still, like one who sleeps in timelessness, at the bottom of the timeless sea,"[4] and that timeless realm is Lothlorien.

Through his gentleness and innate goodness the hero must win the favor of the goddess, who in turn may bestow the "boon of love" upon him, aiding him in his quest by her sanction and blessing. Aragorn admonishes Boromir to "speak no evil of the Lady Galadriel! . . . There is in her and in this land no evil unless a man bring it hither himself" (I, p. 464). As Aragorn knew, the goddess of the quest may possess menacing powers as well as benevolent intentions, and in this capacity acts as temptress to separate members of the Fellowship and to the company's purpose as a whole. She individually tests each adventurer by holding him with her gaze and plumbing his heart, offering silently to each the things he most desires. Commenting upon this interrogation, Boromir echoes the thoughts of the others, "Maybe it was only a test, and she thought to read our thoughts for her own good purpose; but almost I should have said that she was tempting us, and offering what she pretended to have the power to give." Ironically, Tolkien turns this temptation backwards upon the goddess herself when out of devotion and weariness Frodo offers her the One Ring. However, this is not entirely

due to weakness, as Galadriel observes: "Gently you are re-
venged for my testing of your heart at our first meeting. You
begin to see with a keen eye. I do not deny that my heart has
greatly desired to ask what you offer." She recognizes the
growth of heroic potential in Frodo, although he does not seem
aware of it himself. He does not want to see magic in the Mirror
of Galadriel, as does Sam; yet in it he sees the Eye of Sauron and
remains unharmed. Further, Frodo is able to see the Ring Nenya
upon the elf lady's finger when Sam cannot. As universal helper,
the goddess sends the hero away with her blessing. The elves tell
the hobbits, "You are indeed high in the favour of the Lady! For
she herself and her maidens wove this stuff [elvish cloaks]; and
never before have we clad strangers in the garb of our own
people" (I, p. 479). As the travelers drift away from Lothlorien in
their light elfin boats, their vision of Galadriel waving goodby
on the shore directly recalls Campbell's remarks on the nature
of the goddess. To Frodo she already seemed "present and yet
remote, a living vision of that which has already been left far
behind by the flowing streams of Time."

The Road of Trials resumes, this time down the River Anduin. Just above the Falls of Rauros the road reaches a crucial
point. The heroes must go separate ways in accomplishment of
their individual quests, for clearly here two duties call urgently
for the two remaining heroes. Aragorn must journey on to the
defense of Minas Tirith in Gondor, and the Ring must go south
to Mordor. To Sam, faithful helper always at Frodo's side, the
way is "plain as a pikestaff"; yet as the hero, Frodo must decide
which step to take next. This point marks a significant advancement in Frodo's development as quest hero. Even
Boromir's tempting offer to relieve the Ringbearer of his terrible burden and carry it to his beseiged citadel does not sway the
hobbit from the path he knows is right.

The final impetus Frodo needs to make the decision to leave
the company comes from the Ring itself; ironically, this is
another instance in which evil thwarts itself. In attempting to
reveal its presence to the Eye of Sauron, the Ring compels Frodo
to put it on as he gazes across the River towards Mordor. However, in addition to calling the Dark Lord to attention, the Ring
also puts Frodo in touch with other powers equally strong and

receptive to its message; although that power is not named, the reader sensitive to Tolkien's three-in-one quest framework will suspect it is Gandalf, an assumption subsequently confirmed in the narrative. When Frodo slips the Ring on his finger a crux has been reached in his journey and his hero potential receives its first significant test as he experiences the terrible striving of the two powers within him: "He heard himself crying out: Never, Never! Or was it: Verily I come, I come to you? He could not tell. Then as a flash from some other point of power there came to his mind another thought: Take it off! Take it off! Fool, take it off! Take off the Ring!" (I, p. 519). Once he manages to do this, his mind clears at once and he sets himself firmly on the course toward Mordor and the end of the Ring.

Frodo's quest from here follows the Road of Trials in anticipation of atonement with the father or, in more immediately pertinent terms, confrontation with the ultimate dread and fear of Sauron, in fact, to embrace that ultimate power; for Frodo has begun to accept covertly the suspicion that he may not survive beyond the doing of the deed charged to him. This stage of the Road of Trials comprises a series of physical obstacles set in the path of the hero. This is characteristic of the quest myth; it is forward looking, progressive, filled with the initiation symbolism in which irrepairable rifts separate the hero from his past security. Consider Campbell's explanation of this turning point in the Road of Trials:

> The original departure into the land of trials represented only the beginning of the long and really perilous path of initiatory conquests and moments of illumination. Dragons have now to be slain and surprising barriers passed—again, and again. Meanwhile there will be a multitude of preliminary victories, unretainable ecstasies, and momentary glimpses of the wonderful land.[5]

The first barrier facing Frodo and Sam is to win a passage over the barren range of the Emyn Muil mountains ringing the borders of Mordor. Its impassable slopes and crags only begin to forecast the unimaginable peril of the journey facing the hobbits. To its very end Frodo will experience successive phases of near catastrophe and evanescent flashes of illumination until he completes the quest. What appears to be a stroke of luck and momentary relief from their frustratingly slow progress comes as the device of the partial helper Gollum, who agrees to show them the path out of the mountains and into Mordor. This event represents a familiar motif of the quest myth, namely, that acceptance of aid offered along the Road of Trials is risky business, for in the lands of danger and deception it may likely be revealed as yet another form of peril to the hero. Sam's instinctive mistrust of Gollum supports this possibility and causes him to maintain unceasing vigil over Frodo his master. But at this stage of the quest, the Ring has brought Frodo new insight into the nature of suffering and pain; thus he overrides his companion's protests by showing mercy and pity to the wretched former owner of the Ring. He can fully comprehend Gollum's torment.

In the development of Frodo's hero personality, another quality besides compassion begins to take shape at this juncture. In taming Smeagol (Gollum) a newly discovered power suddenly transforms Frodo: "For a moment it appeared to Sam that his master had grown and Gollum had shrunk: a tall stern shadow, a mighty lord who hid his brightness in grey cloud, and at his feet a little whining dog. Yet the two were in some way akin and not alien. . . . Gollum raised himself and began pawing at Frodo, fawning at his knees."

" 'Down! down' said Frodo. 'Now speak your promise!' " (II, p. 285). Is this a new growth of strength in Frodo or something more sinister, specifically, the malevolence of the Ring beginning to show in him? This scene between Frodo and Gollum is preparatory to the insuing episode at the Cracks of Doom in which Frodo falters at the final task, claiming the Ring instead of casting it to the flames, thus forcing Gollum to accomplish its destruction.

The road leads them through the Marshes up into the mountain range surrounding the plain of Mordor where the Dark Tower stands amid the smoke and fumes of the great mountain furnace in which the Ring was forged. The major obstacle encountered here is the Black Gate, or main entrance into the fortress of Mordor. It is shut and perpetually patrolled by orcs and warriors, making entrance from this point impossible. Once again, the quest seems to have reached a cul-de-sac. Tolkien has brought the journey to a halt for a brief episode illustrating what Campbell has termed the momentary glimpse of the wonderful land along the way, the spots of illumination in the path of darkness and dread. Taking an alternative route along the slopes to another secret entrance known to Gollum, the company of three falls in with the skirmish troop of Faramir, captain of Gondor.

From the stronghold hidden behind a waterfall in Ithilien, the ancient pleasure garden of Gondor now overgrown and deserted because of its proximity to the Shadow of Mordor, the hobbits experience a fleeting glimpse of paradise and hope as the setting sun shines through the veil of water covering the mouth of the cave, facing westward: "The level shafts of the setting sun behind beat upon it, and the red light was broken into many flickering beams of ever-changing colour. It was as if they stood at the window of some elven-tower, curtained with threaded jewels of silver and gold, and ruby, sapphire and amethyst, all kindled with an unconsuming fire." As another partial helper, Faramir explains the vision, "This is the Window of the Sunset, Henneth Annun, fairest of all the falls of Ithilien, land of many fountains. Few strangers have ever seen it" (II, p. 358). As if to validate this vision of beauty and hope seen in the west, Faramir, as its representative, gives the hobbits magical walking staves and sets them safely on their way, proving Elrond's prediction about unexpected friendships.

Reluctantly entrusting themselves once more to the guidance of Gollum, Frodo and Sam resume the road into the Mountains of Shadow, making for the secret entrance containing the next obstacle, Shelob's lair. A complex piece of irony is developed here through manipulation of parallels and opposites. Shelob is actually a reverse meeting with the goddess, in evil terms with disastrous results, directly opposed to the episode with Galadriel. She, too, is a female incarnation of the forces of nature so ancient as to be timeless, but manifested as malice rather than benevolence. Of Shelob, Tolkien tells us, "There agelong she had dwelt, an evil thing in spiderform . . . who was there before Sauron, and before the first stone of Barad-dur; and she served none but herself, drinking the blood of Elves and

Men." The pitch darkness of Shelob's lair provides a direct contrast to the light of Galadriel, a relationship of opposites Tolkien impresses numerous times upon the reader. As the darkness of Shelob has relentlessly followed her devotee Gollum, "cutting him off from light and from regret," so the light of Galadriel is ever by Frodo's side, in the form of a phial filled with elvish luminescence distilled from stars ("Far off, as in a little picture drawn by elven-fingers, he saw the Lady Galadriel standing on the grass in Lorien, and gifts were in her hands. 'And you, Ring-bearer,' he heard her say, remote but clear, 'for you I have prepared this.' . . . A light when all other lights go out.") Held aloft, it blazes with increasing brilliance as hope kindles in the hero's mind, another spot of illumination in the darkness of despair.

The escape from Shelob, a momentary respite, is immediately followed by a host of new difficulties to be overcome "again, and again." Confusion threatens the quest as Frodo's capture by orcs guarding the watchtower compels Sam to take the Ring, for the quest must go forward. Another battle must be fought (mostly among the orcs themselves) before Frodo can be rescued by Sam and resume custody of the Ring. The most perilous stage of the quest begins at this point, for essentially the Road of Trials is over in that the hobbits have reached their general destination of the Mountain of Doom, although they have not yet covered the plain that lies before it. From here the struggle is not so much against external obstacles set in their path as it is the Ringbearer's personal tug-of-war between the will of the Ring to return to its master and the forces of good that impel him up the slopes to the Cracks of Doom. The intensity of this conflict saps his strength to the point that Sam is required to carry him. At this low ebb in Frodo's progress, Tolkien begins the preparation for atonement with the father and consequent apotheosis or transfiguration of the hero, the culmination toward which the road has led for so many pages. Frodo's gradual development into the chief heroic character at last reaches maturity, a point where the hero's will becomes set to finish the quest regardless of his own destruction. Frodo "knew that all the hazards and perils were now drawing together to a point:

the next day would be a day of doom, the day of final effort of disaster, the last gasp" (III, p. 267).

Atonement in the mythological context indicates a reconciliation, a coming together of forces and events anticipated throughout the journey of the quest. It occurs when the hero opens "his soul beyond terror to such a degree that he will be ripe to understand how the sickening and insane tragedies of this vast and ruthless cosmos are completely validated in the majesty of Being."[6] The hero-initiate is "divested of his mere humanity" and becomes the vehicle of an impersonal cosmic force, a transition Frodo became aware of when he began to perceive the Ring not as an artifact around his neck, but as a "great wheel of fire" in his mind: "I am naked in the dark, Sam," he says, "and there is no veil between me and the wheel of fire. I begin to see it even with my waking eyes, and all else fades." The will of the hero becomes assimilated in atonement with the forces impelling the quest toward culmination. On the brink of the fiery pit, the takeover is complete. Frodo cries, "I have come . . . but I do not choose now to do what I came to do. I will not do this deed. The Ring is mine!" and sets the Ring on his finger.

In mythic terms, what has just occurred is the paradigmatic pattern of opposition and the attempt at reconciliation, a motif encountered earlier in Frodo's two confrontations with the goddess figure. In this latter case the mythos of the universal mother appeared in both benevolent and malevolent form, each drawing the hero with a fateful fascination. This is now the case with Sauron, the father figure of the overall quest, with the complication "that there is a new element of rivalry in the picture: the son against the father for the mastery of the universe,"[7] in which the struggle for power must result in the annihilation of the two separate entities and the emergence of a single victorious hero figure. This stage of the quest is put in motion as Frodo puts on the Ring, for the Eye of Sauron is instantly aware of him and its whole mind and power becomes "bent with overwhelming force upon the Mountain." The quest is completed as Gollum plunges into the inferno clutching the Ring (obtained through the mythic motif of ritual repetition—Gollum severs Frodo's ringfinger to get it, as Isildur did Morgoth's). With the burden of the quest lifted, the hero returns to himself, "and in his eyes there was peace now."

The narrative lines of the two remaining heroes of the tale, Aragorn and Gandalf, are not as thoroughly detailed as Frodo's in that their quests are complementary to the major quest of returning the Ring to the fire. Nevertheless, their individual courses still follow the paradigms of the Road of Trials, atonement, and apotheosis, occurring at different intervals from those of the major hero, Frodo. Aragorn's initiation is more fully developed than that of Gandalf, whom Tolkien reserves for emphasis of the apotheosis phase. As such, Aragorn's progress in the hero's role follows next in our analysis, with Gandalf rounding out the chapter.

The nature of Aragorn's personal quest and its part in the larger Ring quest are revealed in the council of Elrond. He is chosen to represent Men in the company of the fellowship, because, as Elrond says, "The Ring of Isildur concerns him closely." Following his personal quest, Aragorn wants to take the newly forged sword Anduril into battle to defend the beseiged capital of Gondor, thus reclaiming the throne as the last heir of Isildur of Numenor. But this is not the immediate reason for his inclusion into the Company of the larger quest—as a Ranger familiar with the wastelands of Middle-earth, he is appointed guide for the journey as far as his knowledge extends. This appointment prefigures his developing hero's responsibility, for he is forced to shift from navigator of the trail to sole guide of the quest itself.

Observe, as we did with Frodo, the way in which the heroic capabilities are developed and put to the test in Aragorn, the first test being his assumption of total leadership of the quest through the loss of Gandalf. At this point he is the next most powerful hero, and the leadership falls to him by succession, in spite of his doubts. In the urgency of the moment, when Gandalf slides into the abyss, Aragorn instinctively assumes command to lead them to safety: "Come! I will lead you now!" Aragorn is not the major hero of the larger quest and knows it, but he mistakenly assumes that role to be Gandalf's priority. Like Frodo, Aragorn must somehow resolve his doubts and accept the hero's part suddenly thrust upon him. Each hero reaches this initial crux of confrontation with the duties of the quest; some pass this point practically without thinking, for others it is a step forward in the dark surrounded by doubt. Deprived of Gandalf's powers, Aragorn assumes that the quest must go on without hope.

Aragorn's meeting with the goddess in Lothlorien is more comfortable than it was for Frodo and the rest of his company, for as Haldir tells us, "The name of Aragorn son of Arathorn is known in Lorien . . . and he has the favour of the Lady." The reader will recall that the Road of Trials occasionally allows the hero a momentary glimpse of hope and ecstacy: Aragorn receives such a fleeting vision in Lothlorien as he embraces the memory of his betrothed elf princess Arwen Evenstar, "for the grim years were removed from the face of Aragorn, and he seemed clothed in white, a young lord tall and fair . . . then he drew a breath, and returning out of his thought he looked at Frodo and smiled." Aragorn's rank as hero is acknowledged by Celeborn and Galadriel, for they refer to him now as the leader of the Company, and in bestowing gifts upon the members at their departure for the next stage of the road, Galadriel formally gives him the hero's title and talisman, a green elfstone: "This stone I gave to Celebrian my daughter, and she to hers; and now it comes to you as a token of hope. In this hour take the name that was foretold for you, Elessar, the Elfstone of the house of Elendil!" (I, p. 486). A further vision of hope comes to Aragorn as he guides the travelers down the Great River Anduin to the Falls of Rauros, guarded by two great pillars of stone carved in the likeness of Isildur and his kinsman. The colossal images transfix Aragorn so for a suspended instant he is transformed from the weathered Ranger to a proud sovereign returning from exile.

The sundering of the Fellowship at this point in the road once again requires Aragorn to make a choice of direction as hero: to follow Frodo and aid in the quest of the Ring, to head on toward Gondor with the dead body of Boromir, or to search for the other hobbits captured by raiding orcs. This decision is every bit as crucial for Aragorn as it was for Frodo, both cognizant that the success of the quest may rest on their choices. Aragorn's decision to pursue the orcs and save Merry and Pippin is both rationally and intuitively the right one: "My heart speaks clearly at last: the fate of the Bearer is in my hands no longer. The Company has played its part," and thus the rescue of his friends becomes the motivating element for the direction in which the Road of Trials carries Aragorn and his companions Gimli the dwarf and Legolas the elf.

Setting the second hero on this seeming sidetrack is a significant narrative device, for it allows Tolkien to introduce a previously noted mythic-quest motif, unexpected aid along the way. This is not an insertion of a deus ex machina, however, for the reappearance of Gandalf is organic to the fulfillment of both his personal destiny and the larger quest of the Ring. Gandalf's return also serves as a message-bringing device. He recites a verse sent from Galadriel foretelling the road Aragorn will pursue in his personal quest: ". . . dark is the path appointed for thee:/ The Dead watch the road that leads to the Sea," an allusion to the greatest test Aragorn will be required to face.

The Ranger's immediate road, however, is to keep his promise to return to Rohan and the aid of its ailing king Theoden. Two contests constitute this stage of the journey, one a victory of wits and the other of might. The battle of wits, a common motif among the obstacles put in the path, is joined between the false counselor Grima Wormtongue and the two heroes Aragorn and Gandalf, resulting in the expulsion of Wormtongue. This episode serves both to reinvigorate the aging king of Rohan for his last battle and to set in motion the defense of Minas Tirith in its last stand before the coming tide of Sauron. At every stage now Aragorn's heroic stature increases as his fame spreads through Rohan. His role as warrior-hero is at last openly demonstrated through his contribution to the defense of the ancient mountain fastness of Helm's Deep against Saruman's orcs. "So great a power and royalty was revealed in Aragorn as he stood there alone [on the battered citadel gates] . . . that many of the wild men paused, and looked back over their shoulders to the valley, and some looked up doubtfully at the sky."

The victory at Helm's Deep sets the most perilous phase of Aragorn's journey before him, the Paths of the Dead. In preparation for this undertaking, the heroes are once more the recipients of unlooked-for good luck. As was pointed out earlier, mythic evil often thwarts its own purposes (as in the orcs' quarrel over Frodo, which causes them to massacre each other and allows Sam to rescue his master), thus performing a service instead for the forces of benevolence. In this case the venting of Saruman's rage upon Wormtongue in the Tower of Orthanc causes the evil counselor to throw an object down upon the heads of his captors. The object turns out to be a *palantir*, or seeing stone of great power by which one may cast his sight and thought in many directions and over great distances. Assuming his role as heir, Aragorn states, "Now my hour draws near. I will take it," and bowing in deference Gandalf delivers the crystal globe to him with the interdiction, "Do not then stumble at the end of the road." Thus Tolkien begins to tighten the threads of his narrative, commencing with the solidification of Aragorn's path as the warrior-hero.

Before delving into the final stages of Aragorn's quest, consider the hero's progress toward his goal. Often in the course of the hero's quest he is threatened by very subtle traps in addition to the blatant physical obstacles set in his path, one of the most familiar motifs being the woman as temptress. This type of snare has occurred twice for Aragorn, causing him to temporarily set aside pursuit of his quest. The Company reached Rivendell in late October, but it is not until January, the beginning of the new year, that the quest is actually begun. The days "slipped away" as happiness and contentment settled on each member of the Company, in particular Aragorn, whose lack of motivation to muster the Fellowship may be accounted for in the presence of Arwen Evenstar. At Frodo's first introduction to Elrond he admires the Lady Arwen and "to his surprise Frodo saw that Aragorn stood beside her" and that they conversed privately together. This delay is paralleled in Lorien, when Aragorn tarries in the land of Arwen's birth with the elves of her direct kin. "Here my heart dwells ever," he tells Frodo, referring to Lorien as the "heart of Elvendom on earth." It is a heavy, langorous spell to break, and his delay is lengthy. But as the urgency of his newly defined hero's path presses upon him, Aragorn rejects his third temptation. The Lady Eowyn of Rohan presents him with reason to stay; unable to mask her love for Aragorn, she implores the hero to remain behind rather than take the shunned path where death waits. But the quest has been delayed too long already; thus the hero must be resolute and immediately embrace the road leading to peril and the unknown.

In preparation for this most dangerous stage of Aragorn's quest, comparable to Frodo's last trek across the plain of Gorgoroth to Mount Doom, Tolkien introduces various sources of aid and counsel available to Aragorn before he sets out. First, unexpected help arrives in the persons of Halbarad, a Ranger, and his band, accompanied by the two sons of Elrond. Additionally, supernatural aid comes in the form of messages from Elrond and Galadriel, asking Aragorn to remember the Paths of the Dead, and also from Arwen, who sends with Elrond's sons the great standard of the house of Numenor to be borne in the battle of Gondor, a specific talisman to serve as a token of hope and luck.

Having reached the final stage of the quest, Aragorn, like Frodo, admits that "the time of stealth has passed" and the goal must be won "by the swiftest way." For Frodo this meant a path straight across the plains of Mordor, for Aragorn it is the Paths of the Dead. Yet we must make the distinction here between motivations: Through the palantir Aragorn reveals himself and his reforged sword to Sauron, hoping to protect the Ringbearer by drawing the Enemy's attention. Frodo, on the other hand, simply accepts the impossibility of further secrecy as he and Sam approach the mountain of fire. Aragorn's immediate purpose in treading his perilous course is the enlistment of supernatural aid, a device common to the quest myth. For the purposes of the myth itself, this journey is the supreme test of Aragorn in the hero's role. He rises to the test without hesitation, forecasting a successful end to his labors. Tottering on the edge of madness from fear of the invisible undead legions bidden to follow behind them, the Rangers will themselves to follow him, attesting to his stature as warrior-hero.

In a sense, this last feat is Aragorn's atonement with the father, in that he faces the ultimate fear of his road and conquers it, even employing it to his bidding. This episode, at any rate, prepares Aragorn to approach the physical "father" in Gondor, the Steward Denethor who has ruled the remnants of the empire through the years in which it was thought no heirs of the old kings remained. In this symbolic confrontation, Aragorn must convince Denethor of his right to "rule the universe in his place." He officially proclaims his identity at the siege of the capital Minas Tirith by unfolding to the wind the great standard of the royal house, black with the white tree of Gondor, and "seven stars were about it, and a high crown above it, the signs of Elendil that no lord had borne for years beyond count" (III, p. 150). As further proof of his identity, Aragorn heals the wounds of Eowyn and Faramir, fulfilling the old rhyme that the true king will have the hands of a healer. His lineage is proclaimed a final time in front of the Black Gate of Mordor, as both challenge to Sauron and decoy for the Ringbearer.

With the destruction of the Ring, Aragorn the warrior-hero has also attained the goal of his quest. He has returned to rule in Gondor as the genuine heir of the old kings, and on the day of Mid-summer weds the elf princess Arwen and "the tale of their long waiting and labours was come to fulfillment." Aragorn's apotheosis is detailed for us in the act of his crowning, an event Tolkien foreshadows throughout the bitter journey to victory. The pattern of apotheosis as pursued by the questing hero involves reaching, through mythology, "the divine state to which the human hero attains who has gone beyond the last terrors of ignorance," and further, in universal terms, that "this is the release potential within us all, and which anyone can attain— through herohood."[8] The transfiguration of the hero comes from his total knowledge of good and evil, pleasure and pain, active and passive, yin and yang. Embracing both manifestations through the experience of atonement, the hero emerges as a new, enlightened being in whom opposites are reconciled (for the role of the transfigured hero as giver of the ultimate boon, consult part three of this text). This is the *bodhisattva* way— "living in the world, not retiring to the forest," but instead applying the fruits gained from the quest. The hero is the "sage who, while living in the world, has refused the boon of cessation yet achieved realization, and so remains a perfect knower in the world as a beacon, guide, and compassionate savior."[9] James Frazer iterated this concept of the kingly figure as perfect knower, guide, and savior when he charted the pervasive mythic idea of the "magic of kings"[10] and the sacredness of that office in his study of ancient myth and ritual; we should expect to find this motif in Tolkien's modern myth of Aragorn the King. Throughout the tale the reader is offered signs of his impending rebirth as a young lord of power, superseding the years of trial that have aged his body and spirit in figurative death. The vehicle for this mythic image is the death of the white tree (and with it the line of kings). Further, its renewal gives us a symbol for the reinvigoration of the royal house and lineage with the blood of Isildur's heir and the elvish line of Arwen. What we actually have is Frazer's fertility myth of death and resurrection, the mythic pattern of separation and union, loss and gain. Through the crowning ceremony, the reader witnesses the ritual and mystery of Aragorn's transfiguration from aged exile to king of the new line of Westernesse:

> Then Frodo came forward and took the crown from Faramir and bore it to Gandalf; and Aragorn knelt, and Gandalf set the White Crown upon his head, and said:
> "Now come the days of the King, and may they be blessed while the thrones of the Valar endure!"
> But when Aragorn arose all that beheld him gazed in silence, for it seemed to them that he was revealed to them for the first time. Tall as the sea-kings of old, he stood above all that were near; ancient of days he seemed and yet in the flower of manhood; and wisdom sat upon his brow, and strength and healing were in his hands, and a light was about him. And then Faramir cried:
> "Behold the King!" (III, p. 304)

There is a further extension of opposition worth noting in this ceremony. As noted earlier, Frodo and Aragorn pursue quite different courses as hero—Frodo as the sacrificial savior and Aragorn as the conquering warrior. The contrast is further borne out at the coronation. Frodo is obliged to attend the crowning ceremony in the tattered clothing he had about him when the Ring went to its destruction, as symbols of honor; therefor his own apotheosis is invisible, known only to himself and Sam, who witnessed the events on Mount Doom. But the elf princess Arwen recognizes it, for she bequeathes to Frodo her place in the Grey Havens, thus completing his change from hobbit of the Shire to hero worthy of a place among the Valar of the Havens. In sum, the visual pageantry that opens the reign of the awesome but mortal king becomes an appropriate setting for the unassuming hobbit's boon of immortality.

Following Gandalf through the three-part quest pattern charts his metamorphosis from Gandalf the Grey Pilgrim who amuses hobbits with magic fireworks and green-colored smoke rings into the hero-saint, or world redeemer, the "sage" Campbell speaks of in *Oriental Mythology*. Tolkien does not divulge much information concerning Gandalf's call to adventure and crossing of the first threshold, nor is his journey on the Road of Trials presented with as much detail as in the quests of the other two heroes. This is not where the emphasis upon Gandalf rightly falls; rather, it is on his apotheosis, his transformation through fire and death into the hero's incarnation as the White Rider, a force for good finally equal in power to the evil of Sauron. As Elrond and others correctly note, Gandalf is the prime mover in the success of the Ring quest even though he is not the Ringbearer. He is the cosmic, supernatural hero through whose efforts chaos is averted in the universe. It becomes evident that Frodo's humanly physical journey has served as a paradigm for the higher myth of Gandalf. For this reason Tolkien would have us concentrate upon Gandalf's return to the tale as a being of great power, indispensible in the events of the War of the Ring.

Tolkien joins Gandalf to the quest in the following manner. Through the treachery of Saruman, Gandalf understands what his duty must be: to return to Hobbiton at all cost and perform the test of fire on the bauble he now knows to be the Ring of Power willed by Bilbo to his nephew. This urgent dispatch to Hobbiton is Gandalf's call to adventure, for he promises (although he is not able to keep the promise) to accompany Frodo in his flight from the Shire. Knowledge of Gandalf's difficulty in crossing the first threshold into Rivendell comes as secondary information, so as readers we are as aware of his progress as of the others, but not of his presence. In Bree the travelers receive Gandalf's belated letter of several months previous explaining the possibility of his absence in their departure from the Shire and that he will follow the same route taken by the hobbits. His confrontation with the Black Riders at Weathertop is seen from a distance by the hobbits and reconstructed by them from the signs upon the hill, but again we do not witness the actual event; we know of it only in relation to the journey of the other two heroes. Once they gain the summit of Weathertop the signs of Gandalf's struggle with the enemy are all about: "But in the centre a cairn of broken stones had been piled. They were blackened as if with fire. About them the turf was burned to the roots and all within the ring the grass was scorched and shrivelled, as if flames had swept the hill-top; but there was no sign of any living thing" (I, p. 251). Our final evidence that this has been the site of Gandalf's struggle with Mordor is the discovery of a stone bearing the faintly discernible lines of a G-rune.

Gandalf does not reappear in the crossing of the threshold, but in his characteristic way turns up suddenly where least expected. The first thing Frodo sees as he regains consciousness in Rivendell is "the old wizard, sitting in a chair by the open window." In this interlude between the first threshold of adventure and the departure upon the Road of Trials, Tolkien sheds some light on the nature of Gandalf's own quest through the wizard's explanations to the convalescent hobbit: "There are many powers in the world, for good or evil. Some are greater than I am. Against some I have not yet been measured. But my time is coming. The Morgul-lord and his Black Riders have come forth. War is preparing!" (I, p. 290). This grim fact is iterated by the elf lord Elrond in his naming of Gandalf to the Fellowship, "for this shall be his great task, and maybe the end of his labours." Unlike Frodo, who is unwillingly drawn into the quest, Gandalf actively pursues the hero's path to his own doom.

For Gandalf, meeting with the goddess and atonement with the father occur in reverse order, bringing an end to his Road of Trials much earlier than for Frodo and Aragorn. His fate becomes irreversible once the company agrees to follow him into the Mines of Moria, a fear Aragorn voices in his warning: "It is not of the Ring, nor of us others that I am thinking now, but of you, Gandalf. And I say to you: if you pass the doors of Moria, beware!" (I, p. 388). The testing of Gandalf's powers begins in the goblin pursuit through the depths of Moria, where he is forced to hold at bay a power beyond his present strength, allowing the others to flee further into the recesses of the dwarf ruins. In earlier episodes Gandalf has distinguished himself as the wizard of fire, as when he kindles a tree with a blast from his staff for protection against wargs outside the entrance or battles the agents from Mordor with fire and lightning on Weathertop. Yet this is restrained, calculated display. Gandalf has been holding himself in check so far on the road, but in confronting the unseen terror in Moria he expends all the powers he possesses; yet it is not enough. He has just magic enough to crumble the door behind them: "I have done all that I could. But I have met my match, and have nearly been destroyed. But don't stand here! Go on! You will have to do without a light for a while: I am rather shaken," he tells the breathless troupe. The reader now knows that Gandalf has engaged a mortal enemy, one great enough to drain the wizard's power so his staff, which had been their torch in the tunnels, went dark while "Gandalf felt the ground with his staff like a blind man." The moment of confrontation and atonement comes upon the bridge of Khazad-dûm, where he must once more wield fire to save himself and his friends from the now-visible terror, a man-shaped creature of shadow surrounded by flame and known in Middle-earth as *balrog* (O.E. *bealu*, 'evil,' and *wregan*, 'to arouse').[11] Symbol of primeval fear, the balrog is Gandalf's supreme test, as the Paths of the Dead are for Aragorn and Mt. Doom is for Frodo. Splintering the bridge into fragments with a blinding flash from his staff, Gandalf and his nemesis plunge into the abyss together, there to conquer and be conquered.

As before, Gandalf's activities now move from the realm of immediacy to secondary information. The secondhand report of lightning seen upon Weathertop in Gandalf's initial test of strength is paralleled by the elves' report in Lorien of the effects of his contest with the ancient Terror: "The Dimrill Dale is full of vapour and clouds of smoke, and the mountains are troubled. There are noises in the deeps of the earth," (I, p. 480). The only hint of Gandalf's victory over the balrog comes to Frodo as he peers into the Mirror of Galadriel and sees a figure so like Gandalf he nearly calls the wizard's name; yet the figure is not clothed in grey but in white with a white staff. Gandalf's reentry into the quest, as in previous examples, occurs when least expected. Thinking they have encountered the wizard Saruman,

Aragorn and his two friends interrupt their search for Merry and Pippin to deal with the treacherous wizard, but to their amazement it is not even Gandalf the Grey, it is Gandalf the White, whose "hair was white as snow in the sunshine; and gleaming white was his robe; the eyes under his deep brows were bright, piercing as the rays of the sun; power was in his hand" (II, p. 125). Secondary reporting becomes firsthand, as Gandalf relates the details of his ordeal of "fire and water," earth and sky.

In the process of atonement, the balrog clutches Gandalf to him as they fall, first burning, then freezing as they plunge into dark water cold enough to stop the heart. This is Lévi-Strauss's progression of two opposite forces mediated by another force and finally producing a unity, a single different element, from the process. Out of the depths of the living earth, "where the world is gnawed by nameless things" even Sauron does not know, for they are far older than he, and up the Endless Stair Gandalf pursues his doom to the highest pinnacle of the Silvertine where his enemy is forced to turn and fight for mastery. The Battle of the Peak that insues is now discovered to be the cause of the smoke, thunder, and vapor seen from Lothlorien. The death and rebirth motif is plainly employed here, as Gandalf casts his enemy from the pinnacle and, darkness taking him, "strays out of thought and time" into unknown places. In rebirth he is sent back from oblivion stripped of his former identity as the Grey Pilgrim, and "naked I lay upon the mountain-top," he explains. For the third time the Lord of the Eagles carries him to safety, but on this occasion he is light, nearly transparent, as the original Gandalf has been burned away. Borne by the eagle to Lorien, Gandalf's apotheosis becomes complete:

> Thus it was that I came to Caras Galadon and found you but lately gone. I tarried there in the ageless time of that land where days bring healing not decay. Healing I found, and I was clothed in white. Counsel I gave and counsel took. (II, p. 135)

Now that "Gandalf's head is sacred" and the transfiguration of the hero has been fulfilled, much ahead of the other two heroes, the further deeds of Gandalf constitute his return to society with the boon of his new power, and thus rightly belong to part three of this book.

CHAPTER 5

Unraveling the Design

THIS CHAPTER MARKS PERHAPS THE MOST DIFFICULT PHASE of the journey through the mythic structure of *LOTR*: analyzing the morphological elements of the Second Move of the trilogy, which as we have noted corresponds with the *Initiation*. If it has not become clear by now that "Tolkien's world is as dizzyingly complex and as natural as a snowflake or a spiderweb,"[1] the morphology of the remaining half of the trilogy should convince any recalcitrant disbelievers.

As previously mentioned, *LOTR* is basically a two-move tale of (1) battle and defeat of the villain or his agents, and (2) a difficult task and its solution. The Second Move is complicated, however, by the insertion of two smaller moves centering about the two great battles of this second part: the battle of Helm's Deep against the forces of the White Hand of Saruman, and the seige of Gondor commencing with the battle of the Pelennor Fields against the forces of the Red Eye of Sauron. In this way the complementary quests of Gandalf and Aragorn are merged to augment the larger pattern of the quest of the Ring. The sequential pattern of elements in this Second Move is basically as follows: $(a)A{\uparrow}M[(A\ H\text{-}I)\ (A\ H\text{-}I)]\ N$. Returning to Vladimir Propp, we learn that Division VI of the tabulation of tale functions (Beginning of the Second Move) is a repetition of the sequence of Divisions I through V up to the arrival of the hero, at which point the pattern shifts into Division VII (Continuation of Second Move) containing the paradigm of the difficult task. Further, we discover that the two inserted submoves or subdivisions of the complementary quests also follow the pattern previously outlined for first moves. What follows is a detailed analysis of the Second Move with its divisions and subdivisions in terms of the notation listed in appendix A. Such a graphic sectioning of the narrative pattern will facilitate a better grasp of the overlay design employed by Tolkien to encompass the Ring quest.

Division I. Initial Situation

The spatial-temporal locus is in Rivendell, with the entire Company reunited.

Division II. Preparatory Section

In a reversal, the agents of the hero conduct a reconnaissance of the villain as Elrond sends scouts out from Rivendell to look for signs of the Black Riders.

Division III. Complication

The impetus for the complication is an assimilation of (a) and (A), the lack being the need for a hero to take the Ring to the Cracks of Doom and the villainy consisting of the Enemy's threat of war and destruction of Gondor, an immediate possibility explained by Boromir. Boromir himself functions as the conjunctive element (B^2) by bringing the mysterious rhyme of Faramir's dream to Rivendell for interpretation:

> Seek for the Sword that was broken:
>   In Imladris it dwells;
> There shall be counsels taken
>   Stronger than Morgul-spells.
>
> There shall be shown a token
>   That Doom is near at hand,
> For Isildur's Bane shall waken,
>   And the Halfling forth shall stand. (I, p. 323)

In this way the tale is provided with the motivation for the entry of the hero and the form of his consent, that is, Frodo's simple answer that he will take the Ring. The phenomena accompanying the hero are (1) the delegation of the members of the Fellowship: "The Company of the Ring shall be Nine; and the Nine Walkers shall be set against the Nine Riders that are evil," in which a form of trebling occurs in the designated number of participants; (2) equipage for the journey with the reforged sword Anduril and Bilbo's mail-coat of mithril as well as his old sword Sting; and (3) the charges laid on the hero by Elrond: "The Ring-bearer is setting out on the Quest of Mount Doom. On him alone is any charge laid; neither to cast away the Ring, nor to deliver it to any servant of the Enemy nor indeed to let any handle it, save members of the Company and the Council, and only then in gravest need" (I, p. 367).

The dispatch of the hero follows next, and the Company sets out from Rivendell toward the high pass of Caradhras. The malice embodied in this mountain provides an entry for the function (C), consent to counteraction, for it hurls winds and snowstorms threatening to freeze the Company in their tracks if they do not turn back. They must agree to follow Gandalf into Moria. We find in this function also, a point made previously, that nature itself assumes the role of the catalyst in the determination of events, acting as the motivating force for good or evil, all the while sending the Ring further on its journey. Animate nature here provides the impetus that leads Gandalf to his doom and rebirth and allows the Ring to proceed to Lothlorien untouched.

Division IV. Donors

The journey to the home of the donor consists of the flight from Moria to the golden wood of Lothlorien. A connective element on the way to Lorien is the prophecy contained in the clear depths of the Mirrormere, where the members of the Company see on its surface "plumes of white flame" and "glinting stars" although the sun shines overhead, images suggestive of the emblems of the house of Gondor. The next element of the series is the presentation of the donors, with particular detail given to appearance: "Very tall they were, and the Lady no less tall than the Lord; and they were grave and beautiful. They were clad wholly in white; and the hair of the Lady was of deep gold, and the hair of the Lord Celeborn was of silver long and bright; but no sign of age was upon them, unless it were in the depths of their eyes; for these were keen as lances in the starlight, and yet profound, the wells of deep memory" (I, p. 459).

In preparation for the transmission of a magical agent, the donor Galadriel offers her Mirror (a repetition of the Mirror-mere element) in which Frodo receives prophecies of the journey and proves himself worthy of her gifts by turning the testing back upon the donor herself as we noted in chapter 4. The trebling of auxiliary elements is prepared for in the revelation of one of the Three Elvish Rings of Power, Nenya the Ring of Adamant. The donor gives magical agents to each of the members of the Company to suit his particular needs or desires; the star-glass to Frodo, the Elfstone to Aragorn, the box of Lothlorien earth to Sam, a bow to Legolas, a lock of Galadriel's hair to Gimli, and gold and silver belts to the others. Further, the Company is provided with light elf-boats, rope, elvin cloaks and *lembas*, or waybread, for times of need. The donor functions (F^3) the Agent is Made to Order and (F^4) Advice are included here, as well as (J^2) Recognition of the Hero, Aragorn.

Division V. Entry of Helper to Arrival of Hero

The inclusion of the helper at this point in the sequence, Division V, is the arrival of Gollum, clinging to a piece of wood floating down the river behind the travelers. The swift current of the Anduin delivers the Company to their appointed place (G^4), the lookout seat of Amon Hen on a hill overlooking the water. Here the motivating element is Boromir's threat to the Ring, forcing Frodo to put it on to escape him. This incident completes the sequence of Division VI.

Division VII. Continuation of the Second Move

The first function of Division VII is (0), the unrecognized arrival of the hero, in which the Eye of Mordor is attracted to Frodo when he puts on the Ring but passes over him as he slips it off just in time. This function is also the motivating factor for the ensuing separation of the Company, as Frodo and Sam set off for

Mordor while the others are seized with a kind of "madness," which sends them running pell-mell and calling for Frodo in loud voices. Trebling also occurs here in that the leadership of the quest has moved on to the third hero, Frodo, having begun with Gandalf and shifted to Aragorn. This function ($<$), Parting of Ways, is important here for it suspends the progress of the major quest and allows the intrusion of the first subdivision: the complementary quests of the two heroes Aragorn and Gandalf against Saruman. This same function will signal the entrance of the second submove as well.

Subdivision I. Complementary Quests of the Two Heroes

The motivating villainy in Subdivision I is the attack of Saruman's orcs with some accompanying spies from Mordor upon the Company, Boromir's slaying, and the capture of the two remaining hobbits. Dispatch of the hero occurs in Aragorn's decision to let the Ringbearer go his own way and instead try to rescue Merry and Pippin, the function (Pr). The conjunction occurs in the approach of the Riders of Rohan, who inform the "Three Hunters" (trebling again) about their slaughter of the orc party in question. Function (B^3) also serves as the motivation for the continuation of the search. Counteraction (C) comes in the decision to search for the hobbits in Fangorn, which eventually leads them to the magical helper, Gandalf the White. Backtracking, Merry and Pippin also undertake a journey to the home of the donor when the raiding orcs carry them to the edges of Fangorn Forest. The attack of Rohan on the orcs (Rs) allows the hobbits to slip into the wood, where they meet the donor, Treebeard. Preparation for the acquisition of magical aid (F) takes place at the Entmoot, where the Ents, shepherds of trees, agree to march on Isengard. Again the powers of nature take form as motivating characters. Treebeard, the prime mover in this episode, carries the hobbits to the seige of Isengard in the crooks of his limblike arms, performing the function (G^2). These last two functions are repeated for the sphere of action of Aragorn and his friends. The magical helper (Gandalf) reveals himself to them (F) (T^1), motivating their ride to Edoras (G).

Gandalf and Aragorn are received in the Golden Hall of

Theoden (entry of the helpers), precipitating three connective and motivational incidents: the overthrow of Wormtongue (X, exposure of false counselor or hero), restitution of Theoden (K^1, breaking a spell), and recognition of the hero Aragorn (Q). These three functions are the motivating forces for the ensuing battle of Helm's Deep, because through their effects Theoden once more wants to defend his land and wants to regain his tarnished glory in combat, a step Wormtongue had prevented him from taking.

Battle with the agents of the villain (Saruman, at this point in the submove) around the natural fortress of Helm's Deep ends in victory for the Rohirrim with the unexpected arrival of Gandalf and the enchanted trees of Fangorn (H-I). The ride of the victors to Orthanc, the tower of Saruman, is the connective element for a repetition of the previous functions, only this time it is the sequence (H^2I^2), a contest of wits and the hero's superiority over his challenger. The voice of Saruman casts a spell upon his captors, causing them to see him as the hero, rather than Theoden or Aragorn or Gandalf, until the latter steps forward revealed as the White: "I am Gandalf the White, who has returned from death. You have no colour now, and I cast you from the order and from the Council. . . . Saruman, your staff is broken" (II, p. 241), exposing him for his treachery (X). Thus the sequence H-I is repeated for the forces of the villain, and then for the villain himself, a technique we shall observe in the second submove as well. This last vicious confrontation is the motivating element for a most important function (Y, Transmission of Signalling Device): in his rage Wormtongue flings down at the victors the palantir by which Saruman has communicated with Mordor. This object itself serves as a motivation when foolish curiosity overcomes Pippin, compelling him to steal it from the wizard and peer into it where the Eye of Mordor catches him, to its detriment as we shall discover:

> The air seemed still and tense about him. At first the globe was dark, black as jet, with the moonlight gleaming on its surface. Then there came a faint glow and stir in the heart of it, and it held his eyes, so that now he could not look away. Soon all the inside

seemed on fire; the ball was spinning, or the lights within were revolving. Suddenly the lights went out. He gave a gasp and struggled; but he remained bent, clasping the ball with both hands. Closer and closer he bent, and then became rigid; his lips moved soundlessly for a while. Then with a strangled cry he fell back and lay still. (II, pp. 251–52)

Once again, evil has defeated itself, for Wormtongue's thoughtless action causes the Eye to believe the Ringbearer may be captured in Orthanc, drawing its attention further away from the truth. Thus Gandalf is motivated to leave the rest of the hosts of Rohan and ride with the speed of the wind upon Shadowfax, carrying the stunned hobbit to Gondor. The end of this episode moves the tale back into the main Division VII.

The function introduced next is (*M*), the Difficult Task, with all the obstacles and aid necessary to reach its completion. Frodo and Sam's crossing of the Emyn Muil Mountains is doomed to failure without the aid of the helper Gollum, drawn into the tale once more. With his guidance, they are able to make a safe although precarious passage through the Dead Marshes, where only the spider-footed Gollum can find a path. Several auxiliary elements are trebled at this point; the quest once more has three main participants, and three times the winged horrors, the Nazgul, fly over them, presaging doom to Gollum, "Three times!" he whimpered. "Three times is a threat. They feel us here, they feel the Precious. The Precious is their master. We cannot go any further this way, no. It's no use, no use!" (II, p. 306). An unexpected helper on this road is Faramir, who gives the hobbits a glimpse of Ithilien and bestows on them gifts and advice for their further advancement of the quest. He bids them turn their attention to nature, as it reflects and seemingly aids the will of the Enemy, "A waiting silence broods above the Nameless Land. I do not know what this portends. But the time draws swiftly to some great conclusion. Storm is coming. Hasten while you may!" (II, p. 384). The journey to the Crossroads follows (*G*) as Gollum heads for his secret entrance into Mordor.

The ancient powers of nature become an operant force in the structure again, here in the form of Shelob, previously referred to in the *Initiation* section of chapter 4. She is an inversion

of the "focal figure of all mythology and worship,"[2] the goddess
Earth and her manifestations, her fertility and bountifulness
turned to evil as "far and wide her lesser broods . . . spread from
glen to glen." The element (J^1) occurs again, as Frodo narrowly
escapes a mortal wound from the giant spider's sting. The
wounding is motivation for Sam to carry on the quest by himself
(trebling in the decisions made by Aragorn, Frodo, and now
Sam to lead the quest forward). A forecast of Frodo's transfiguration is seen in his face as Sam removes the Ring, for it
became "fair of hue again, pale but beautiful with an Elvish
beauty, as of one who has long passed the shadows." Here also
parting of ways (<) marks the point at which the second submove is inserted, in this case the battle of Gondor against the
Lord of the Nazgul.

Subdivision II. Complementary Quests of Two Heroes

The second subdivision is the most complex section of the
narrative design, for Tolkien applies several transformations
and inversions to the standard ordering of a first-move sequence. Here is the actual linear sequence of events : (BC ↑)
$DEF\ A^7$ ($PrRs$) BC↑ H-$I\ X\ Q$↑Rs. In unraveling these threads, the
functions must be presented in their standard ordering, thus
isolating clearly the elements juggled to present simultaneous
though separately located events in the action.

Villainy: The Red Arrow, declaration of war, comes from
Mordor to Gondor and thence to Rohan (A^7).

Connective elements paralleled: Pippin enters the service of
Denethor of Gondor as the armies are gathered in the walled
citadel, while Merry swears fealty to Theoden during the muster
of Rohan. Pippin here makes an observance of the role of animate nature in the events, as it forecasts the battle to come: ". . .
the sky had grown ashen-grey, as if a vast dust and smoke hung
above them, and light came dully through it. But in the West the
dying sun had set all the fume on fire, and now Mindolluin stood
black against a burning smoulder flecked with embers. 'So ends
a fair day in wrath!' he said" (III, p. 50). Gandalf puts it more
directly: "The Darkness has begun. There will be no dawn."

Conjunctive moment: Halbarad the Ranger arrives unlooked for, with the sons of Elrond (B^3, Entrance of Intermediaries). They provide the motivation for the next function (C).

Counteraction: The sons of Elrond bring messages for Aragorn that convince him to take the Paths of the Dead although it is a last resort (C).

Dispatch: Taking leave from Eowyn at Dunharrow, Aragorn and the small troop of Rangers with Legolas and Gimli take the trail up the Haunted Mountain (↑).

This sequence of (BC ↑) is repeated in the ride of Rohan to the aid of Gondor: (B) Pukel Men offer aid against the orcs of the Enemy, (C) Rohirrim consent to take the savages' shortcut, and (↑) the troop races toward the besieged city. Here the forces of nature again exert a tangible influence in the unraveling of events, in this particular instance both as a foreshadowing device and as the final crucial element that turns Gondor's defeat into victory: One of the scouts of Rohan brings news that "the wind is turning," bringing a fresh sea breeze out of the south with the promise of light at dawn instead of the Great Darkness.

Donors: Aragorn takes the haunted pass to the Stone of Erech where he calls upon the restless shades of the oathbreakers to follow him and fulfill their duty as warriors of Isildur. They agree, silently following his troop, leaving a wake and rumor of fear as they pass (DEF).

Transportation to appointed place: Aragorn's company takes the black ships of the Corsairs of Umbar to reach Gondor in time (G), aided by the fresh wind from the sea noted in the sequence (BC ↑).

Another set of magical donors and helpers comes to Gondor in the person of Gandalf and Faramir, racing for the gates of the city with the Nazgul in pursuit (forms of arrival, FGPr). This scene serves as motivation for the second appearance of the villain of this particular submove, the Lord of the Nazgul. For the third time (trebling) Gandalf faces directly an individual agent of the powers of darkness, ordering it to stand aside: "You cannot enter here. . . go back to the abyss prepared for you! Go back!" Rescue comes at this critical moment with the horns of Rohan sounding up the fields of the Pelennor (Rs).

Here the sequence *H-I* is repeated, as before, for the agents of the villain and then for the villain himself:

Battle with agents of villain: The fight on the Pelennor Fields (*H*).

Victory over agents: As Rohan has done earlier in the day, Aragorn comes unexpectedly to the aid of the besieged city, bringing with him the Rangers and troops from the coastal principalities. Nature facilitates the victory here, as the very weather Sauron had marshalled to confound his adversaries turns against him and "the darkness was breaking too soon, before the date that his Master had set for it: fortune had betrayed him for the moment, and the world had turned against him; victory was slipping from his grasp even as he stretched out his hand to seize it" (III, p. 139), function (*I*).

Battle with villain: The Nazgul king strikes down the king of Rohan and wounds his daughter, disguised as Dernhelm the soldier (*H*).

Victory: Eowyn destroys the Nazgul whom no man could harm (*I*).

Exposure of false hero or counselor: Denethor's madness and attempted treachery (an element trebled by the treacheries of Saruman and Boromir) ignite his own funeral pyre, as evil thwarts evil (*X*).

Recognition of hero: Aragorn's ability to heal by the use of *athelas*, or kingsfoil, (*Q*) reveals his royal blood.

The complementary quests begin to merge with the larger quest when victory is won in Gondor and the battle ended. Two connective and motivating incidents bring about this merger. In a repetition of the Council of Elrond, the lords of Gondor hold council upon how best to aid the quest of the Ring, deciding finally to proceed openly as a great host to the Black Gate in hopes of drawing the Eye away from its inner fortress where the Ringbearer still labors, function (↑). At the Black Gate Sauron's human spokesman, the Mouth of Sauron, presents the heroes with the mithril shirt of Frodo, motivating Gandalf to challenge the hosts inside Mordor to come out and do battle.

Unexpected rescue by the eagles serves as the connecting link that transfers the action back into the sphere of the major quest.

The difficult task (continued) picks up with Sam's rescue of Frodo from the Tower of Guard when the orcs' quarrels work to their detriment as usual. Sam says of the hundred or so orcs he had to deal with, "But they've done all the killing of themselves. That's lucky." Continuing the task (M), Sam and Frodo cross the plain of Gorgoroth.

The resolution of the difficult task (N) is brought about by the motivating element of Frodo's putting on the Ring at the last moment and claiming it for his own. For a final time evil defeats itself, as the power of the Ring that causes men to lust after it becomes the instrument of its unmaking: Mad Gollum, having previously borne the Ring, cannot control himself as Frodo claims it and thus bites off the hobbit's ring finger, falling into the fire at the same time, marking the hero (J^1) for the third time (trebling).

Rescue (RS^1, Hero is Carried Through Air) of Sam and Frodo from the ruin of Mordor is again accomplished by Gwaihir, the Lord of the Eagles. The transfiguration element for Frodo means emerging from under the spell of the Ring into himself once more, sadder but wiser so to speak. His transfiguration is completed through the singing of the "Lay of Nine Fingered Frodo" celebrating his fame for all time (T^4, Change in Reputation).

Beneath this linear sequence outlined above lies another network of patterns hinted at in the brief mention of various motivating forces, particularly nature and evil. This is the domain of Lévi-Strauss, to be taken up in the following and final chapter of the *Initiation*.

CHAPTER 6

Binary Opposition in Middle-Earth

THE KEY TO MYTHIC STRUCTURE and by extension the structure of the mind, in the words of Claude Lévi-Strauss, is "binary opposition" and the dynamic relationship between the poles of the opposition that achieves mediation or unity, a conclusion repeatedly emphasized in his work *The Savage Mind*. Picture the symbol for the yinyang in which the two opposite halves form a complete sphere; both opposing elements are necessary for wholeness, making them paradoxically complementary as well. In abstract terms this process of mediation is necessary in the production of myths, for the "elements of mythical thought" lie halfway between images and concepts, namely, in signs or mythical symbols. "One understands then how mythical thought can be capable of generalizing and so be scientific, even though it is still entangled in imagery. It too works by analogies and comparisons," always formulating new arrangements of elements in the mythical structure.[1] Thus mythical thought abides in the "events and experiences which it never tires of ordering and reordering in its search to find them a meaning." Human existence is reflected in the paradigmatic patterns intrinsic to mythic thought, as we have suggested in the preceding chapters, and indeed we may observe these processes at work in *LOTR*.

The successful blending of opposites is often requisite for the representation of genuine human experience. In Tolkien's trilogy we find this clearly emphasized not only in the overriding imagery of light and dark, black and white, good and evil, but by direct statement as well, as in the effect of the lay of Frodo sung to the victorious hosts of Gondor: "And all the host laughed and wept . . . until their hearts, wounded with sweet words, overflowed, and their joy was like swords, and they passed in thought out to regions where pain and delight flow together and tears are the very wine of blessedness" (III, p. 286). In the actual process of mediation, two opposite examples of the same species coming together through some power or agent of mediation emerge as a single new entity, which has the potential to split again into opposites, perhaps at some distant time.[2] Thus the malevolent and benevolent forces clash in confrontation in the Third Age of Middle-earth; yet it is not for the first time ("It was Gil-galad, Elven-king and Elendil of Westernesse who overthrew Sauron, though they themselves perished in the deed. . . . Then Sauron was vanquished . . . until his shadow took shape again in Mirkwood" [I, p. 83]), nor for the last ("Always after a defeat and a respite, the shadow takes another shape and grows again"). Out of the peace won through the clash of opposing forces will some day come a need for a new hero to vanquish a newly risen evil. As the result of the mediating process, the structure of the trilogy remains both varied and constant. Tolkien emphasizes this pattern by first letting Bilbo explain it to Frodo, who later repeats it for Sam's benefit: "Don't adventures ever have an end? I suppose not. Someone else always has to carry on the story"; "No, they never end as tales . . . but the people in them come, and go when their part's ended" (II, p. 408). This pattern is an intrinsic element of mythology itself, as Joseph Campbell indicates in *Oriental Mythology*:

> Strife is an element in the universe which cannot be ignored; Seth is perennially subdued by Horus but never destroyed. Both Horus and Seth are wounded in the struggle, but in the end there is a reconciliation: the static equilibrium of the cosmos is established. Reconciliation, an unchanging order in which conflicting forces play their allotted part—that is the Egyptian's view of the world and also his conception of the state.[3]

Both the forces of good in the trilogy (the High Elves and their Three Rings of Power) and the forces of evil (Sauron and his agents) are reconciled in the same fate of destruction brought on by the mediating event of the Ring's destruction.

This same pattern operates on numerous smaller scales in *LOTR*, particularly between individual characters. Gandalf and the balrog are two opposing forces that, through the mediation of the power struggle, emerge as a new being, Gandalf the White, the White Rider whose "head is sacred." This same paradigm helps clarify the relationship between Gollum and Frodo. Both are of the hobbit species, yet opposite in character; however, they are reconciled through ownership of the Ring, forcing them both to play the hero's role (Frodo for carrying the Ring to the Fire, and Gollum for taking it into the flames). Out of this merging of opposing forces occur life and death. On an even more individual level, two opposing forces war within the same being, as in Gollum and Smeagol—Slinker and Stinker, Sam called them. Once again the force of the Ring subdues the latter personality for the former, so the quest may be carried to completion. What we have charted here is the paradigm as familiar to mythologists as a password—the cycle of death and rebirth. Out of the death of the Third Age with its Elvish magic is born the Age of Men. The bitter winter of battle gives way to victorious spring for the men of Westernesse who have "passed through the darkness and fire to a new day."

It becomes evident that Tolkien's imagination works in opposites from the numerous examples of this relationship between persons and objects in Middle-earth. The two wizards, Gandalf and Saruman, offer such a contrast. Both are of the same species, sorcerers of great power, yet of opposing motivations. Thus Gandalf's benevolence enables him to conquer his nemesis in Moria whereas Saruman's lust for the Ring and personal power becomes his doom. This force of the Ring works similarly upon another pair of binary opposites. Faramir and Boromir are brothers, yet very unlike in character. Boromir succumbs to the influence of the Ring; however, Faramir has the strength to reject it when he learns it has come into his hands through Frodo. He tells the Ringbearer, "Fear not! I do not wish to see it, or touch it, or know more of it than I know . . . least peril perchance waylay me and I fall lower in the test than Frodo son of Drogo." In like manner, the two kings of men, Theoden and

Denethor (who although technically the Steward of Gondor rules it as a king), operate within the pattern. The evil of Sauron works upon both; yet Theoden with the aid of Gandalf throws off the spell and rides to a glorious death, while Denethor is crushed, attempting to burn his remaining son alive on the pyre that becomes his own. Thus as Theoden is laid on a bier of honor in the throne room of Gondor, Denethor breaks the Steward's staff over his knee amid the flames of the Tombs.

As a final example we may offer the relationship of Shelob and Galadriel, both manifestations of the dread power of the female nature, yet binary opposites in Tolkien's conception. The former relies on the power of darkness for the purposes of malice, yet is as necessary to the balance of the natural world of Middle-earth as the elvish queen's uplifting powers of light. Total reconciliation, then, comes from a movement forward from the ruins of confrontation, from spiritual and physical death to rebirth. Returning to Lévi-Strauss, we observe down the long line of ages that "mythical worlds have been built up, only to be shattered again, and that new worlds were built from the fragments,"[4] through the mediation process. Turning from the "fragments" of Mount Doom, we look with Frodo toward the new age, its promise of endurance and strength tempered by the blend of opposite elements inherent in Middle-earth.

PART THREE
RETURN

CHAPTER 7

Pulling
the Threads Together

WE COME NOW TO THE FINAL PHASE OF THE CIRCLE of the mythic quest, which requires "that the hero shall now begin the labor of bringing the runes of wisdom . . . back into the kingdom of humanity, where the boon may redound to the renewing of the community, the nation, the planet, or the ten thousand worlds."[1] However, the return to the community may be of either a negative or positive form. If the hero in his triumph has won the blessings of the supernatural powers extant at the end of the quest, these patrons will insure his safe and comfortable route home. Conversely, if he must accomplish the quest through the deception of malevolent guardians, as when Jason stole the Golden Fleece from under the claws of the sleeping dragon, he must take flight for his life, in which he will require nefarious "help from without" to accomplish a dubious return. Since all three of Tolkien's heroes make a return of the first type, it becomes clear, especially in Frodo's case, that the assisting powers of nature that furthered the progress of the quest also facilitate the homeward journey. In crossing the return threshold, the hero most often finds that both he and the world he left have changed, and part of his process of return is to reshape himself into a member of that community; sometimes this cannot be done, and the hero must once again leave the community after bestowing his boon.

Having recuperated in Gondor until May, Frodo finally expresses the wish to make the return journey: ". . . the days are running away, and Bilbo is waiting; and the Shire is my home,"

a home he once believed was lost to him forever. Yet the desire
to return stems not only from homesickness but also from hints
of things not right at home. Sam's glimpse in the Mirror of
Galadriel suggests trouble in Bag End, and the fact that tobacco
from Hobbiton turns up in the storerooms of Orthanc engenders
further misgivings: "It's time we got back," says Sam.

The ultimate boon of peace and goodwill bestowed on
Middle-earth by the destruction of the Ring is clearly reflected
in the world of nature as it shows the new spring, brightening
their return trip. The blighted land itself undergoes a transfiguration, sending forth the most plentious and beautiful of
springs the inhabitants of Middle-earth could remember. With
the threat of evil removed, at least for some time to come, the
world of nature breathes deeply once more, and as the slow
leisurely trip back to Rivendell stretches into summer various
helpers along the road bid farewell to the Company. "September came in with golden days and silver nights"; yet in the midst
of the tranquility a blight remains; Frodo has changed too much
to return to the life he left. His wounds have left him perma-
nently marked, and the "Elvish air" so many had noticed in him
is now manifested strongly as he voices a sudden craving for the
Sea and the Grey Havens. Gandalf tries to comfort him, explaining that some wounds "cannot be wholly cured," to which
Frodo responds, "There is no real going back. Though I may
come to the Shire, it will not seem the same; for I shall not be the
same. I am wounded with knife, sting and tooth [trebling], and a
long burden. Where shall I find rest?" (III, p. 331). For Frodo
crossing the return threshold into Hobbiton is an ominous
event, with wind and rain of autumn at his back, for the Shire
has become the last refuge of evil for the cruel men and half-orcs
of Saruman. The final boon, then, is the defeat of these intruders
along with the death of Saruman at the hands of
Wormtongue—again evil defeats itself.

The succedent restoration of the Shire parallels the transformation wrought in the wide world of Middle-earth through
the promise of spring. It is important here to realize why the
quest reaches its final phase in autumn rather than spring:
Spring is the time of promise and potential, and autumn is
harvest time, when the fruits of one's labors are brought to

culmination and completion. Although Frodo has to live with the suspicions of his neighbors due to his mysterious absence and sudden heroic return, he now becomes, as Joseph Campbell would say, the "master of two worlds," able to cross the threshold between his own lands and those of far away kingdoms, as well as receiving outlandish visitors of all sorts. But he still cannot fit into the old world, for his wound from the Nazgul blade always brings back the darkness upon the anniversary of its occurrence. He finally has to admit that he cannot live his old life in Hobbiton. Thus Frodo fulfills Arwen's desire that he should take her place in the Grey Havens, and the hero of the Ring quest passes from Middle-earth.

Frodo is not the only hero of the three who gives up his right to remain in the human world. Gandalf, as prime mover of the Age of Elves and Wizards, must now pass into the twilight of "Elvenhome," for he is the keeper of one of the Three Rings of Power, Narya the Great, which must also fade from Middle-earth with the destruction of the One Ring. But we are getting ahead of ourselves, for Gandalf's actual return to the world after the accomplishment of apotheosis is not at Hobbiton but much earlier, during the great battle of Minas Tirith against the forces of evil. This is the boon that Gandalf brings back to Middle-earth—his new power as the White Rider able to confront the Morgul lord at the gates of Gondor and raise the seige of that walled city, as well as thwart the designs of Sauron at the Black Gate. Repeatedly throughout the long struggle with the armies of Saruman and Sauron, Gandalf arrives unexpectedly, bringing hope and rescue to the beleaguered forces, always proving stronger than his enemies. At Helm's Deep he arrives at the rear of the conflict with the shadowy hosts of Fangorn at his heels, bringing death upon the orc warriors as hope suddenly surges in the hearts of the men of Rohan: "The White Rider was upon them, and the terror of his coming filled the enemy with madness," exactly as the wickedness of the Nazgul lord could drive to madness the warriors of good, through fear. But once the battle is done and the Ring cast to the flames, the great age of magic is past and Gandalf, too, is no longer needed; his duty is fulfilled.

It is Aragorn, King of the Age of Men, who remains in the

world as a symbol of might and justice. His return to the world with the boon of leadership comes after he has successfully traversed the Paths of the Dead, calling up that dread company as allies in the last desperate fight. He, too, brings such fear to the enemy boarding the ships at the shore of the Great River that they fling themselves into the water to drown. Aragorn's return to the world he left is thus accomplished by crossing the return threshold in the black ships of the enemy to the rescue of Eomer and the Rohirrim on the plains of the Pelennor; the boon he brings is victory in arms and the beginning of a new line of kings in Gondor, sprung from the old blood of Westernesse. He also becomes master of two worlds by reuniting the lineage of men and elves in his marriage to Arwen Evenstar. His acceptance back into the world of men is a joyous and acclaimed occasion, with the citizens of Gondor welcoming him with open arms and hearts as their king. Aragorn will remain in Middle-earth, as will his elfin bride.

There is a threefold pattern here in the return of the heroes. Each must return to do battle a final time to end his quest: Gandalf in Rohan, Orthanc, and Gondor as well as Mordor; Aragorn in Gondor and Mordor besides the battle for the fleet of the Corsairs; and Frodo in Hobbiton. We find also that the three hero lines reach atonement and return at spaced intervals in the chronology of the narrative, Gandalf first, then Aragorn, and finally Frodo. The pattern may be indicated in this way, each beginning with the dispatch from Rivendell:

Gandalf: (↑) . . . . . (Moria)——→ (Return to Rohan)
Aragorn: (↑) . . . . (Paths of Dead)——→ (Return to Gondor)
Frodo: (↑) . . . . (Mt. Doom)——→ (Return to Shire)

This scheme brings us to a final investigation of the morphology of Tolkien's trilogy, which is actually a continuation of the larger Second Move discussed mainly in part two. The discussion stopped with the function (*T*), for it was here that the *Initiation* phase as outlined previously came to an end, with apotheosis and the resulting ultimate boon. The analysis resumes now with the last part of Division VII.

Division VII. End of Second Move

The element (*W*) Wedding and Accession to Throne occurs first, in the marriage of Aragorn and Arwen on Midsummer's Day, after his coronation with the crown of Elendil. The other two heroes then must set out on their own return journeys, heading as a group first for Rivendell. Early in the trip back they come upon the two slovenly figures of Saruman and Wormtongue. Instead of smiting the spiteful pair dead in their tracks from his wrath at their treachery, Gandalf pardons and spares these two remaining villains (*U neg*, Villain is Spared), which will later prove to be the motivation for the third submove of the tale, occurring in the Shire.

With the parting of ways (<) the Company leaves the entourage from Lorien at the borders of the enchanted wood, passing on through Rivendell and so to the Shire where the final parting comes when Gandalf informs them he is not going into the Shire with them. His parting speech neatly summarizes the myriad examples demonstrating this phase of the quest and the concomitant passing of the Third Age; all the threads of the hero's role, his duty and his rewards, are bound up here:

> I am not coming to the Shire. You must settle its affairs yourselves; that is what you have been trained for. Do you not yet understand? My time is over: it is no longer my task to set things to rights, nor to help folk to do so. And as for you, my dear friends, you will need no help. You are grown up now. Grown indeed very high; among the great you are, and I have no longer any fear for any of you. (III, p. 340)

With the departure of Gandalf, the four adventure-worn hobbits make for the bridge into Hobbiton, returning by the same path over which they fled a year ago (↓), and thus the quest comes full circle. It is here that the final battle with evil must be fought, and in this way the pattern reaches the third subdivision.

Subdivision III. "Scouring of the Shire"

The villainy in Subdivision III is the wreck and pillage of Hobbiton's sleepy prosperity by the ruffians and other agents of Saruman, and their threats of violence to the two Ringbearers and the two hobbit warriors of Gondor and Rohan.

The conjunctive movement takes the form of (B^2) Announcement of Misfortunes, for the local hobbits forced to guard the returning heroes finally drop their pretenses and tell all about the blight fallen on the Shire. This is the motivation for (C), Counteraction to the dictates of the usurpers. The captains Merry and Pippin now come to prominence as they lead the rising of the Shire-folk against the agents of "Sharkey," whom they discover to be Saruman himself. In a battle with the ruffians the hobbits show unexpected courage and ferocity under the leadership of their new captains, defeating men twice their size $(H\text{-}I)$. This victory marks the end of the subdivision and the resumption of Division VII.

Division VII. (Continued)

Saruman himself is made to face his adversaries after the defeat of his evil henchmen, along with the ever-present shadow Wormtongue. Here punishment finally comes to the remaining villains of the tale $(U,$ Punishment of Villain) as Wormtongue stabs his master and is himself filled instantly with hobbit arrows.

The resolution of the Second Move is (W^4) and secondarily (W): A marriage takes place between Sam and his sweetheart Rose, and shortly following Frodo leaves for the Grey Havens, where the final parting of ways takes place. He boards the white ship with Gandalf, Elrond, and the folk of Lorien, and to his surprise, Bilbo.

A final look over this portion of the morphology reveals a major trebling not obvious earlier in the analysis. The three submoves correspond to the points of return and final conflict for each of the three heroes. The first submove was the battle of Helm's Deep, which marked the return of Gandalf as the White Rider; the second submove consisted of the seige of Gondor, which was the point of return for Aragorn; and as we have just shown, the third submove presented the final battle fought in the tale as Frodo returns to the Shire. One can now realize how Tolkien has beautifully balanced and conceived the mythical structure of *The Lord of the Rings*.

CHAPTER 8

Patterns in
the Deep Structure

IN SURVEYING THE FRAMEWORK OR SURFACE STRUCTURE of *LOTR* the reader recognizes how "dizzyingly complex" it is; by probing below this linear framework we also see it is indeed as natural "as a snowflake or spiderweb," not only in the treatment of nature itself but also in the grouping of paradigms that become more obvious through careful analysis. This is where we discover Tolkien's "rebirth of the numinous" or mythic consciousness noted earlier from Stanley Hopper's essay. This sense of the numinous is presented through animate nature, from which a sentient power surfaces to provide guidance, hindrance, prophecy, and direct intervention. This immanence is dramatized rather than explained, as in the personification of the ancient powers of the forest through the creature Treebeard or of the earth in the evil spider form Shelob, or even more impressive, the seasonal powers personified in Tom Bombadil. These sentient beings of nature are actual characters; however, the powers of weather and land also show sentience in manipulating the course of events, again pointing up the natural magic inherent in the world. The inhabitants of Middle-earth do not need any "outside reference" or authorized instruction to reach the "divine": they are in it and they are it.

One finds this very idea explicated by Alan Watts, who speaks of an "organic image of the world, the world as a body, as a vast pattern of intelligent energy that has a new relationship to us. We are not in it as subjects of a king, or as victims of a blind process. We are not in it at all. We *are* it! It's you."[1] This motivational "intelligible energy" surfaces as the malice of the mountain Caradhras, which forces the Company to take the alternate route through Moria. In Moria it takes the form of the balrog, a manlike shape of shadow and fire, an ancient buried power of the earth existing long before Sauron laid the stones for the tower of Barad-dur. Further, the hobbits are surrounded by this natural energy in the land of Lorien, where the winter is as beautiful as spring and just being there heals the traveler of fear and fatigue. Absorbing this power of the elves, Sam explains, "I feel as if I was *inside* a song, if you take my meaning." We have already mentioned Treebeard, as personification of the powers of nature. He is referred to by the elves as "Eldest" with great awe and respect. Through his energy the great forest of Fangorn is roused, as nature crushes its offender Saruman.

The land itself reflects the intelligible powers residing in it, for although the blighting power of the Enemy has spread over much of the lands stretching away from Gondor, still in pockets of goodwill and safety spring peeps through, as in the dales of Fangorn where Merry and Pippin catch a "fleeting vision" of the rebirth of nature. Again, in the land of Ithilien where the Ringbearer meets Faramir, some vestige of the promise of another spring is visible, for this slim border of land is still held by the men of Gondor against the Dark Lord. When the Ring is destroyed the land undergoes a transformation into greenery and flowers, as if the spring had been held in check and suddenly set free. On the other hand, the land itself becomes evil under the shadow of the Dark Lord, and its malice engulfs the hobbits as they attempt to cross it, causing in them physical sensations of fear and sickness. The Emyn Muil, cruel range skirting the wastelands outside Mordor, receive crashing torrents of rain as chasms gape open in the path of the hobbits like no other mountains they have yet scaled. Fear is on every side, accentuated by the passing of the winged Nazgul high overhead. Yet far more ominous is the region of Mordor itself. In one incredible passage of description, Tolkien reveals nature in its evil manifestation:

> The air, as it seemed to them, grew harsh, . . . here neither spring nor summer would ever come again. Here nothing lived. . . . The

gasping pools were choked with ash and crawling muds, sickly
white and grey, as if the mountains had vomited the filth of their
entrails upon the lands about. High mounds of crushed and
powdered rock, great cones of earth fire-blasted and poison-
stained, stood like an obscene graveyard in endless rows, slowly
revealed, in the reluctant light. . . . A land defiled, diseased beyond all healing. . . . "I feel sick," said Sam. Frodo did not speak.
The sun broadened and hardened . . . but even the sunlight was
defiled. (II, p. 302)

This land of horror is in direct contrast to the beauty just
observed in the land of Lorien, where goodwill prevails.

Goodwill and ill will are also manifested in the various
aspects of weather and atmosphere of Middle-earth, in the air
and sky. War and the coming strife are prophesied and reflected
in the elements, as in the tense silence that hangs over the
Nameless Land while the hobbits tarry with Faramir. In the
failing light of the sunset, the distant peaks of Gondor are red
stained, forecasting bloodshed and war. The actual intervention
of natural forces in the events of the war occurs in the coming of
the Great Darkness, which sends its cloud of gloom over the sky
at sunset, shutting out light and hope as it passes over Gondor
and reaches its fingers toward the mustering forces of Rohan.
Here nature is Mordor's messenger, and the message is war:
Theoden is told, "It comes from Mordor, Lord . . . from the hills
in the Eastfold of your realm I saw it rise and creep across the
sky, and all night as I rode it came behind eating up the stars.
Now the great cloud hangs over all the land between here and
the Mountains of Shadow; and it is deepening. War has already
begun" (III, p. 89).

Farther on the elements of air and sky and light become
agents of goodwill, for the dawn comes several times at crucial
moments to inspire the forces of good with hope and courage.
With the sounding of the great horn of Helm at the Battle of
Helm's Deep, the orcs are driven back and the king of Rohan
rides forth to meet them as "light sprang in the sky, Night
departed," assuring victory. A parallel incident occurs in Gondor when the seige at the gates looks darkest: a cock crows to
greet the morning "that in the sky far above the shadows of
death was coming with the dawn," just as the horns of Rohan

announce their entrance into the battle before the gates of Gondor. Nature's most pivotal intervention in the battle, however, is the unexpected wind that rises from the sea and drives the gloom before it. The Darkness breaks and scatters too soon, as fear dissipates with the morning light: The forces of good in nature successfully challenge the immanence of evil, paralleling as well as manipulating the world of men. With the pall of the Enemy dispersed, nature prophesies the victory of Gondor and her allies; "the fire in the sky was burning out." Aragorn reads the sign aloud, "Behold the Sun setting in a great fire! It is a sign of the end and fall of many things, and a change in the tides of the world" (III, p. 167).

A further mythic aspect of animate nature is the power in names, a potency immanent in the world of Middle-earth. Time and again companions on the road caution each other not to speak evil names or the language of Mordor aloud for fear of calling the power down upon themselves. The reverse is true as well, in which the names of elvish heroes long past are called aloud for protection, as when Frodo unknowingly shouts the name of Elbereth when the Morgul king stabs him on Weathertop, a charm that Aragorn credits with saving his life. This supposed power in naming is one of the imprints of experience discussed by Joseph Campbell. The myth consciousness in man recognizes the "audible aspect" of nature as well as the visible; thus the pronouncement of the name of a natural power "will cause him to appear and his force to operate, since the name is the audible form of the god himself," demonstrating the notion of "participation."[2]

So great is the power of the names of evil things that to speak them at night or on the open road is to invite disaster. Even the creatures of Middle-earth with powers of their own such as Gandalf and the elves hold the evil names of power in awe and do not trifle with them. In Hobbiton Gandalf refuses to explain his errand to Frodo until the morning, saying that "such matters were best left until daylight." The elves Frodo meets on the road through Hobbiton on the first night of his departure speak in hushed voices when asked about the Black Riders on their trail. "We will not speak of this here," says Gildor. The reader will recall the effect of the language of Mordor spoken

aloud at the council of Elrond, even though the words are
uttered deep in the center of Elvendom. Also in Rivendell, the
foolish Pippin recklessly calls Frodo the "Lord of the Ring,"
bringing an instant admonishment from Gandalf to the effect
that "Evil things do not come into this valley; but all the same
we should not name them. . . . We are sitting in a fortress.
Outside it is getting dark" (I, p. 298). Even Gollum, who has
passed in and out of Mordor more than once, is afraid to name
the powers to whom he has bowed; his voice sinks barely above
a whisper as he tells Frodo and Sam of his secret path through
the tunnel of Shelob, and of the dreaded Silent Watchers that
guard the pass on the other side. Indeed, Gollum refuses to say
the name of Sauron, referring to him only as the "Master" or the
"Black One." In like manner the men of Gonder refer to Mordor
as the "Nameless Land," and Faramir speaks of "servants of the
Nameless" rather than of Sauron. Faramir is careful even in his
reference to the Ring, not naming what it is but rather calling it
"Isildur's Bane," acknowledging only that Isildur in his time
"took somewhat from the hand of the Unnamed." This power in
names is not confined to the influence of Sauron, but applies as
well to other powers of malevolence in Middle-earth, as when
Gollum would not speak Shelob's name. We observe this fact
also when the sons of Elrond bring to Aragorn Galadriel's message to take the fearful Paths of the Dead. Having delivered their
message to Aragorn upon the plains at night, Elrohir warns,
"But let us speak no more of these things upon the open road."
Even Gandalf, when asked how he fared with the balrog in
Moria, exclaims, "Name him not!" for Gandalf now understands him to be one of the great, ancient powers of the earth
beyond the evil of Sauron.

However terrible and ominous the evil influence of these
names of power may appear, the naming of elvish and Numeno-
rian heroes and objects of magic serve just as strongly for the
forces of good. Numerous times the utterance of elvish names
saves the speaker from danger; yet again we may point out that
the elves are not the only powers in nature that may be called
upon through naming; for example, Tom Bombadil also serves
this purpose. Frodo's first rescue in this manner is through the
naming of the queen of Elvenhome beyond the Western Seas,

Elbereth-Gilthonial, by the elves of Gildor's party; yet in times to come the hobbits themselves will call the name both intentionally and unconsciously. The song of the approaching elves of Gildor's company sounds through the night air in Hobbiton just in time to ward off the black shape crawling up the back of the road towards the petrified Frodo. He recognizes them as High Elves, for they speak the name of Elbereth. As we have previously observed, at the attack upon Weathertop Frodo's life is saved from the blade of the Morgul king, for when the wraith lunges at him Frodo "heard himself crying aloud: O Elbereth!" Aragorn observes that the stroke of Frodo's sword did little but slash the hem of the Black Rider's robe, while "more deadly to him was the name of Elbereth." In Mordor both Sam and Frodo call upon the elvish name for protection. In the tunnel of Shelob, Frodo clutches the phial Galadriel had given him and cries an elvish charm, not knowing what he has spoken at all, as if another voice had repeated the charm through his own. This same phenomenon happens to Sam as he fights a desperate battle with Shelob; he touches the same phial and cries "Gilthonial A Elbereth!" drawing enough courage and spirit to mortally injure the great spider. A third time the elvish names give power to Frodo and Sam, as they speak the names in the Tower of Cirith Ungol, snapping the will of the Silent Watchers long enough to slip quickly through the gates into the valley of Mordor.

A further display of this animate power in the names of nature and her creatures can be discovered in the function of Tom Bombadil, Tolkien's perfect personification of the powers of nature under investigation. He can sing up the powers of wind and weather, stars and clouds, trees and earth, and cold stone upon the barrow downs, as well as the silent void of space in a time far before the dimmest memories of the hobbit folk. Out of sudden awe and fear at the realization of such mastery, Frodo asks him, "Who are you, Master?" Tom's reply is both simple and confounding, for he *is* nature in Watts's terms; thus his origins and powers must remain obscure to us, while the manifestations of his potency are readily observed. "Don't you know my name yet? . . . Eldest, that's what I am. Mark my words, my friends: Tom was here before the river and the trees; Tom remembers the first raindrop and the first acorn . . . he knew the dark under the stars when it was fearless—before the Dark Lord came from Outside" (I, p. 182).

So ancient and untouchable is the natural power of Bombadil, infused with the cheery heedless energy of spring, that the Ring has no power over him, and his country is an island of safety from the Darkness growing all round its boundaries. In him we see the power of naming at its most effective, first when the hobbits call for help from the wiles of Old Man Willow, himself a formidable power in the natural world of the Withywindle Valley. The call for help almost instantly brings Tom singing along the shore, and his song is a charm that dissipates the spell of the willow: "I know the tune for him," Tom tells the distraught hobbits. "Old grey Willow-man! I'll freeze his marrow cold, if he don't behave himself. I'll sing his roots off. I'll sing a wind up and blow leaf and branch away. Old Man Willow!" Similarly, when the hobbits make ready to leave the house of Tom and his lady Goldberry, the River's daughter and herself an agent of nature, Tom teaches them a rhyme to sing should they fall into danger:

> Ho! Tom Bombadil, Tom Bombadillo!
> By water, wood and hill, by reed and willow,
> By fire, sun and moon, harken now and hear us!
> Come, Tom Bombadil, for our need is near us! (I, p. 186)

The charm proves effective against the fatal spell of the barrow wights who hold the hobbits prisoner in their deathly tombs. Frodo's last ounce of strength is expended in singing the charm, and in answer he soon hears the muffled sound of Tom's singing, ". . . Tom, he is master:/ His songs are stronger songs, and his feet are faster," as the stones of the crypt fall away, letting in the sunlight. Much later in the quest, for the third time (trebling) the mention of Tom's name brings inspiration and rescue to Frodo and Sam as they face terror in the pitch black of Shelob's lair. Sam is reminded of the darkness of the barrow from whence he got the small blade he carries by his side, and thinks, "I wish old Tom was near us now!" Instantly he perceives a light growing in his mind and finally remembers the star glass given to Frodo in Lorien, the phial containing the light of the heavens long familiar to Tom Bombadil. Tolkien cannot make more explicit for us the "participation" and immanence of the "divine" in nature. He has achieved for his readers an authentic rebirth of the numinous in the myth consciousness.

This use of the power in naming is an example of what Claude Lévi-Strauss terms the "rites of control" or the positive and negative acts aimed at increasing or restricting the phenomena of the numinous. Thus the "disjoined past of myth" or the mythic consciousness finds expression "through biological and seasonal periodicity."[3] This idea of flux brings us to the final set of patterns observable in the mythic structure of Middle-earth, namely, the seasonal cycle, in which is reflected the cycle of ages in Middle-earth and the repetition of the waxing and waning of good and evil, with its concurrent and recurrent need for a hero. Thus myth unites the opposites of past and present, as well as future, and of permanence and impermanence: "mythical heroes can truly be said to return, for their only reality lies in their personification; but human beings die for good."[4]

Mythic imagination, then, is both diachronic and synchronic, pulling the two opposing views together into a unified world attitude; this is the operation of the mythic impulse discussed at the outset of our journey through the work of Tolkien. Campbell's delineation of this phenomenon is in terms of the "Cosmogonic Round," by which he means that "all the visible structures of the world—all things and beings—are the effects of a ubiquitous power out of which they rise, which supports and fills them during the period of their manifestation, and back into which they must ultimately dissolve."[5] Greater and lesser rounds are contained within the Universal round, as in the pattern of movement from deep sleep to waking noted in chapter 1 of this study, also in the paradigm of birth-death-rebirth, and the movement through the seasons of the year. This image of the circular paradigm is universally consistent to the mythic mind. The American Indians were sensitive to it, and we find an explanation of the cosmogonic round remarkably pertinent to our own purpose in the words of the old Sioux medicine man, Black Elk:

You have noticed that everything an Indian does is in a circle, and
that is because the Power of the World always works in circles, and
everything tries to be round. . . . The sky is round, and I have
heard that the earth is round like a ball, and so are all the stars.
The wind, in its greatest power, whirls. Birds make their nests in
circles, for theirs is the same religion as ours. The sun comes forth
and goes down again in a circle. The moon does the same, and
both are round. Even the seasons form a great circle in their
changing, and always come back again to where they were. The
life of a man is a circle from childhood to childhood, and so it is in
everything where power moves.[6]

In the saga of the Third Age of Middle-earth one finds
constant mention of the greater and lesser cycles of the cosmogonic round: in the continual need for a hero to mediate the
conflicts of good and evil; in the developing ages of Middle-
earth; in the seasonal cycle of the particular quest of the Ring;
and ultimately in the general pattern of the quest myth—
separation, transformation, reunion. The forces of evil and good
are in continual alternation through the cycles of years. For
example, in the First and Second Ages an evil entity took shape,
of whom Sauron was a mere servant, before the Ring was ever
conceived, and in the Third Age, although Sauron is reduced to a
shadow as the Ring is unmade, there is no assurance the shadow
will not take shape again in some distant time and place. Elrond
describes this fact at the council, recalling the years and ages
preceding their own: "It recalled to me the glory of the Elder
Days and the hosts of Beleriand, so many great princes and
captains were assembled. And yet not so many, not so fair, as
when Thangorodrim was broken, and the Elves deemed that
evil was ended for ever, and it was not so" (I, p. 319). Inevitably,
Frodo repeats the actions of his predecessor Bilbo, who also set
off on a quest unknowingly related to the present one. Gandalf
tells him, "You take after Bilbo. . . . There is more about you
than meets the eye, as I said of him long ago." We have already
mentioned Frodo's observance on this point that the "great
tales" themselves never end, only the people in them come and
go.

Thus the tale passes from the Third Age of Elves and
Wizards into the Age of Men, which holds its own promise

distinct from that which passes away. The wanderers reached Lothlorien in its winter; yet the coronation of Aragorn and the ensuing reinvigoration of the ancient line of Numenor takes place in May. The promise of spring is embodied in the sapling of the White Tree planted anew in the citadel of Minas Tirith in place of the one withered for so many years as the line of the kings failed. The diurnal cycle prevails here as well, for it is significant that the newly crowned king enters the gates of his palace on the "Eve of May" and "with the rising of the Sun." As we have noted many times previously, nature reflects and illustrates the forces operating in the world, a point made by Treebeard: "For the world is changing: I feel it in the water, I feel it in the earth, and I smell it in the air." This sense of the universal round is best expressed by Gandalf in his farewell to Aragorn:

> This is your realm, and the heart of the greater realm that shall be. The Third Age of the world is ended, and the new age is begun; and it is your task to order its beginning and to preserve what may be preserved. For though much has been saved, much must now pass away; and the power of the Three Rings also is ended. And all the lands that you see, and those that lie round about them, shall be dwellings of Men. For the time comes of the Dominion of Men, and the Elder Kindred shall fade or depart. (III, pp. 307-08)

The cycle is renewed, with the initial situation of prosperity and well-being at the beginning of the new kingdom, which may wait a long time for the first act of villainy that will set a new hero once more upon a quest. The quest of the Ring, on the diachronic level, which began in autumn at the failing of the year, passing into a winter of battle and despair, moves toward completion in the promise of the new spring and the harvest of a second autumn. One almost gets the sense of passing backward through time, for the Company reached the safety of Rivendell in October when the quest begins, and in the return this original group tarries in Rivendell until October to pass the same ford at the river that came to their aid a scant year ago. So also did Bilbo's quest exhibit a circular shape, backtracking over the same territory in the return, with Bilbo finally becoming aware of the departure-return cycle himself; in his poetry he realizes that "Roads go ever ever on" and "feet that wandering have gone/ Turn at last to home afar" (*Hobbit*, p. 284). The quest is completed, the tale has come full circle, and the desire of the psyche for unity and wholeness, the sense of the completion, is satisfied once more. Here lies the work of the true mythmaker, who through the mythic impulse has brought to light a new validation of the primal patterns existing below the surface of consciousness. This is Tolkien's achievement.

Epilogue:
Tolkien as Mythmaker

EARLY IN THE TEXT MENTION WAS MADE OF Joseph Campbell's idea
that the mythogenetic zone for our times is the individual
human heart and psyche, that interior world of the individual
where he confronts his own spirit or Buddha nature, as distinct
from the synchronic existence that places the individual in
community, nation, and world in the sequence of history. Taking this concept further in the light of the foregoing analysis, the
artist drawing upon the creative imagination must look to this
first world of the self and the myth consciousness for material
and experience that will ring true to the practiced ears of
twentieth-century listeners. This is the role of the artist, to
summon "our outward mind to conscious contact with ourselves." To do this successfully today the artist must become
receptive to the mythic impulse and its sources. He must
"communicate directly from one inward world to another, in
such a way that an actual shock of experience will have been
rendered: not a mere statement for the information or persuasion of a brain, but an effective communication across the void
of space and time from one center of consciousness to another."[1]

The center of Tolkien's consciousness is Middle-earth; yet
its inner consistency and the universal values of courage, hope,
endurance, and compassion touch each of us in our own centers
of being, hopefully stimulating our creative imaginations in the
myth-building process. Thus a reading of Tolkien's trilogy is an
experience rather than an intellectual exercise. He successfully
dramatizes rather than explicates the age-old patterns of

mythic thought and knowledge. Vicariously experiencing Frodo's struggle up Mount Doom puts us in contact once again with the essential human need for love and support, for the loss of identity in the merging of kindred spirits where separate personalities are doomed to failure: Frodo and Sam become one, a single will striving for the completion of the impossible task even beyond hope, taking motivation only from the combined effectiveness of their spirits. Frodo says to Sam when the task is finished, "I am glad you are here with me. Here at the end of all things, Sam." After we have lived with the elves, men, and hobbits through the draining experiences of the War of the Ring, we can share in the joy and relief that comes after. We are satisfied through the primal pattern of peril and rescue, intense strain and release, labor and reward. That the world of Middle-earth seems real to so many readers of Tolkien's subcreation does not appear surprising in this light, for the experiences of the characters are universally valid, no matter how other-worldly their trappings may be. As we have emphasized, the specific elements of the myth are subject to variation; yet the structure and pattern remain constant. Whether the seeker is Odysseus, Stephen Dedalus, or Frodo, the validity and truth of the quest lie within each of us, in the mythic consciousness.

To successfully revitalize the mythic process for modern readers, the artist-mythmaker must himself believe in the elements with which he is working. He must feel that the myth of the quest is valid and capable of being completed with new meaning for each individual, a conviction that will shape the artist's work into a document of fulfillment, or frustration if it is lacking. If the artist himself has felt the impact of the unity gained through the quest cycle, the products of his imagination will reveal the positive course of the completed circle. This source of unity is often denied to us by modern writers who become engrossed only with the Road of Trials, with the sufferings along the way of men unable to carry themselves beyond their immediate misfortunes to the confrontation and apotheosis necessary for wholeness. These authors, as well as the characters of their works, offer no boon to society, no token of hope or renewal. The only course left to them is to "lie down in darkness."

In looking back over the "dizzyingly complex" fabric of *The Lord of the Rings*, as we have analyzed it, it is a simple matter to determine that Tolkien has fulfilled the four functions of myth delineated earlier, proving himself a valid mythmaker for the modern world. He has awakened us once more to a recognition of the numinous, a sense of "at-one-ment" with the world and nature enjoyed in the deep wells of the mythic consciousness. In so doing he has also rendered for his readers a total view of the universe of Middle-earth and, by extension, our own. This universe has order within chaos, evidenced through the pattern of opposition and mediation. The social function is served as well, for Tolkien internally validates a moral order universal to all men, rather than insisting upon a didactic external prescription of the right way to live. In other words, instead of moralizing about the corruptness of men and their damnation through their sins, demanding that one must be good and turn the other cheek in face of adversity, Tolkien has Frodo show compassion for the miserable Gollum on the barren crags of the Emyn Muil so we believe in it. He demonstrates barbarism through the nature of orcs and their consistent quarreling and defeating of their own purposes. The temptation and fall of Boromir is more eloquent than many sermons and the receptions given the travelers in Rivendell, Lothlorien, Rohan, and Gondor reveal more about nobility of character than we might glean from a treatise upon social order and decorum. A desirable social order is demonstrated in the establishment of the line of Aragorn, set up to promote justice and nobility in the years to follow. Finally, as we have pointed out, the psychological function is served through Tolkien's valid presentation of the spiritual quest and of the way in which it may stimulate the reader to reach into his own creative imagination and inner resources for the discovery of self and the worth of self. He sets the individual in perspective with (1) the world about him and the power of the universe immanent in it, (2) his temporal existence in his immediate company, and (3) his own inner identity. This is the ultimate boon the author has brought back from his journey into the imagination.

Thus the artist as mythmaker is, in Tolkien's words, a "subcreator," a maker of a world consistent with itself and with the creatures who move about in it, which makes its message valid for those who experience this subcreation through the printed page. As Claude Lévi-Strauss puts it, "he [the artist] is thereby transformed into an active participant without even being aware of it. . . . he feels himself to be their creator with more right than the creator himself."[2] The trilogy has been liberally quoted in the text, not only to provide evidence for the analysis, but also to aid the reader who has followed the developing theses in becoming an "active participant" in the events of the quest. For an involvement in both the quest myth of the trilogy and in this analysis of it is really the same. We arrive full circle in both cases, in each striving to reach unification and completion. In this way one attains the psychic uplift that is the "ultimate boon" of the creative imagination, whether it be applied to subcreation or study.

APPENDICES

APPENDIX A

List of Abbreviations

	Preparatory section
α	Initial situation
β	Absentation of elders
γ	Interdiction, command
δ	Breaking of interdiction
ϵ	Reconnaissance of villain about hero

A	*Villainy*

A^1	Threat of cannibalism
A^2	Threat of murder
A^3	Seizure of a magical agent or helper
A^4	Casting of a spell
A^5	Capture and imprisonment
A^6	Plundering, theft
A^7	Declaration of war

a	*Lack*

a^1	Lack of an individual (helper, hero, etc.)
a^2	Lack of wondrous objects

B	*Mediation, the conjunctive incident*

B^1	Call for help
B^2	Announcement of misfortunes
B^3	Entrance of intermediaries
B^4	Singing of a lament or lay

C	*Consent to counteraction*

$\uparrow$	*Departure, dispatch of hero*

D	*Donor*

D^1	Test of hero
D^2	Greeting, interrogation
D^3	Combat with hostile donor

E	*Reaction of hero to donor*
E neg	Negative reaction
F	*Acquisition of magical agent*
F^1	Agent is found
F^2	Agent appears of its own accord
F^3	Agent is made to order
F^4	Agent is intangible, advice, a rhyme, etc.
G	*Transference or guidance of hero to designated place*
G^1	Hero flies through the air
G^2	Hero rides, is carried
G^3	Hero is led
G^4	The route is pointed out to hero
H	*Hero struggles with the villain*
H^1	Open combat
H^2	Contest of skill, wits
I	*Victory over the villain*
I^1	Victory in open battle
I^2	Superiority in contest
I^3	Expulsion of the villain
J	*Marking of the hero*
J^1	Hero is wounded
J^2	Token is worn on the body
K	*Misfortune relieved*
K^1	Breaking of a spell
K^2	Release from captivity
K^3	Resuscitation
M	*Difficult task*
N	*Solution to task*

O	*Unrecognized arrival of hero*
Pr	*Pursuit of hero*
Pr^1	Attempt to destroy hero
Pr^2	Attempt to capture
Q	*Recognition of hero*
Rs	*Rescue of hero*
Rs^1	Hero carried through air
Rs^2	Intervention of helpers
T	*Transfiguration*
T^1	New physical appearance
T^2	New clothes
T^3	Effect of enchantment
T^4	Change in reputation
U	*Punishment of villain*
U neg	Villain is spared or pardoned
W	*Wedding and accession to throne*
W^1	Monetary reward at denouement
W^2	Other position of rank awarded
W^3	Promise of marriage
Y	*Transmission of a signalling device*
<	*Leave-taking or parting of ways*
↓	*Return of the hero*
mot.	*Motivations*
+	*Positive results of a function*
neg	*Negative results of a function*

§   *Connectives*

⋮   *Trebling*

APPENDIX B

Schemes of the Tales

The Hobbit:

α γ a² [B⁴ DEF G⁴] ↑ A¹ (D³F¹) §/ A⁵ B H-I § / A³ F neg (F²)
H²-I² / A² Pr H-I Rs¹ § G¹ D² / a¹ (a⁴) H-I </ A⁵ M-N : / A⁶ H-I / A⁷
(a²) § F neg H-I / W¹↓ Q X

The Lord of the Rings:

  I. α β ε ↑ A² (pr) § B (Rs)< C § [B A⁵ K⁸] DEF [A⁵ B¹ H-I K⁸] §
    G³ : A² (Pr) H-I J¹ G² § (Pr) Rs²
  II. α ε neg A⁷ (a¹) B² : ↑ C<D¹ E : F³,⁴ (J²) § G⁴ : O< :
  III. A² : (Pr)↑BC (Pr) G § (Rs²) DF § G² [F (T¹) § G²] K¹ (XQ) [H-I
    H²-I² § Y (F)]
  II. (continued) M § : G J¹ : <
  IV. [(B³ C↑) DEF A⁷ (PrRs)] B³ C↑H-I XQ↑Rs :
  II. (continued) M-N X mot. Q J¹ : Rs¹ : T³ W U neg<↓
  V. A B² C H-I
  II. (continued) U W (W⁴) <

Notes

PROLOGUE

1. Claude Lévi-Strauss, "The Structural Study of Myth," *Journal of American Folklore*, 68 (1955): 444.
2. Alan Dundes, "Introduction," *Morphology of the Folktale*, by V. Propp, trans. Laurence Scott, 2nd ed., rev. and ed. Louis A. Wagner (Austin and London: University of Texas Press, 1968), p. xv.
3. Joseph Campbell, *Creative Mythology*, vol. IV (New York: The Viking Press, 1968), pp. 4–6.
4. Ibid., p. 677.
5. Ibid.
6. J. R. R. Tolkien, ed., *Sir Gawain and the Green Knight* (Oxford: Oxford University Press, 1925), p. xvi.
7. Lévi-Strauss, "The Structural Study of Myth," p. 430.

CHAPTER ONE

1. Joseph Campbell, *The Hero With the Thousand Faces* (New York: Pantheon Books, 1949), p. 130.
2. Campbell, *Hero*, p. 256.
3. Ibid., p. 22.
4. Ibid., p. 266.
5. Joseph Campbell, *Creative Mythology*, vol. IV (New York: The Viking Press, 1968), pp. 647–56.
6. Joseph Campbell, "Mythological Themes in Creative Literature and Art," in *Myth, Dreams, and Religion*, ed. Joseph Campbell (New York: E. P. Dutton and Co., 1970), p. 148.
7. James Joyce, *A Portrait of the Artist as a Young Man* (New York: The Viking Press, 1965), pp. 252–53.
8. Vladimir Propp, *Morphology of the Folktale*, trans. Laurence Scott, 2nd ed., rev. and ed. Louis A. Wagner (Austin and London: University of Texas Press, 1968), pp. 21–23.
9. Ibid., pp. 119–127.
10. Stanley Romaine Hopper, "Myth, Dream, and Imagination," in *Myth, Dreams, and Religion*, ed. Joseph Campbell (New York: E. P. Dutton and Co., 1970) p. 116.
11. Campbell, *Creative Mythology*, p. 677.
12. Hopper, "Myth, Dream, and Imagination," p. 119.
13. Ibid., p. 125.
14. Ira Progoff, "Waking Dream and Living Myth," in *Myth, Dreams, and Religion*, ed. Joseph Campbell (New York: E. P. Dutton and Co., 1970), p. 177.
15. Hopper, "Myth, Dream, and Imagination," p. 136.

CHAPTER TWO

1. J. R. R. Tolkien, "On Fairy-stories," *The Tolkien Reader* (New York: Ballantine Books, 1966), p. 10.

2. Ibid.

3. For linear diagrams and schema of the plots, including morphological notation, see appendices at the end of this volume.

4. Vladimir Propp, *Morphology of the Folktale*, trans. Laurence Scott, 2nd ed., rev. and ed. Louis A. Wagner (Austin and London: University of Texas Press, 1968), p. 85.

5. W. H. Auden, "Good and Evil in *The Lord of the Rings*," *Critical Quarterly*, 10 (1968): 141.

6. J. S. Ryan, "German Mythology Applied—The Extension of the Literary Folk Memory," *Folklore*, 77 (Spring 1966): 47, 54.

CHAPTER THREE

1. Joseph Campbell, *Creative Mythology*, vol. IV (New York: The Viking Press, 1968), p. 3.

2. Ibid, p. 4.

3. J. R. R. Tolkien, "On Fairy-stories," *The Tolkien Reader* (New York: Ballantine Books, 1966), pp. 58–59.

4. William Ready, *The Tolkien Relation* (New York: Paperback Library, 1968), p. 34.

5. Lévi-Strauss, "The Structural Study of Myth," *Journal of American Folklore*, 68 (1955): 431.

6. The three books of the trilogy are referred to subsequently in the text as I, II, and III.

7. Vladimir Propp, *Morphology of the Folktale*, trans. Laurence Scott, 2nd ed., rev. and ed. Louis A. Wagner (Austin and London: University of Texas Press, 1968), pp. 104–6.

8. Tolkien, "On Fairy-stories," pp. 25–26.

CHAPTER FOUR

1. Joseph Campbell, *Primitive Mythology*, vol. I (New York: The Viking Press, 1959), p. 50.

2. Ibid., p. 54.

3. Joseph Campbell, *The Hero With the Thousand Faces* (New York: Pantheon Books, 1949), p. 97.

4. Ibid., p. 111.

5. Ibid., p. 109.

6. Ibid., p. 147.

7. Ibid., p. 162.

8. Ibid., p. 151.

9. Joseph Campbell, *Oriental Mythology*, vol. II (New York: The Viking Press, 1962), p. 280.

10. James G. Frazer, *The New Golden Bough: A New Abridgment of the Classic Work by Sir James George Frazer*, ed. Theodor H. Gaster (New York: Mentor Books, 1964), pp. 34, 93, 289–92.

11. J. S. Ryan, "German Mythology Applied—The Extension of the Literary Folk Memory," *Folklore* 77 (Spring 1966): 50.

CHAPTER FIVE

1. Peter S. Beagle, "Tolkien's Magic Ring," in *The Tolkien Reader* (New York: Ballantine Books, 1966), p. xi.

2. Joseph Campbell, *Occidental Mythology*, vol. III (New York: The Viking Press, 1964), p. 7.

CHAPTER SIX

1. Claude Lévi-Strauss, *The Savage Mind*, trans. by George Weidenfeld and Nicolson Ltd. (Chicago: University of Chicago Press, 1966), pp. 19–21.

2. Ibid., pp. 67–8.

3. Joseph Campbell, *Oriental Mythology*, vol. II (New York: The Viking Press, 1962), p. 83.

4. Lévi-Strauss, *Savage Mind*, p. 21.

CHAPTER SEVEN

1. Joseph Campbell, *The Hero With the Thousand Faces* (New York: Pantheon Books, 1949), p. 193.

CHAPTER EIGHT

1. Alan Watts, "Western Mythology: Its Dissolution and Transformation," in *Myths, Dreams, and Religion*, ed. Joseph Campbell (New York: E. P. Dutton and Co., 1970), p. 22.

2. Joseph Campbell, *Primitive Mythology*, vol. I (New York: The Viking Press, 1959), pp. 85–86.

3. Claude Lévi-Strauss, *The Savage Mind*, trans. by George Weidenfeld and Nicolson Ltd. (Chicago: University of Chicago Press, 1966), p. 236.

4. Ibid., p. 237.

5. Joseph Campbell, *The Hero With the Thousand Faces* (New York: Pantheon Books, 1949), p. 257.

6. John G. Neihardt, *Black Elk Speaks* (New York: Pocket Books, 1972), pp. 164–65.

Epilogue

1. Joseph Campbell, *Creative Mythology*, vol. IV (New York: The Viking Press, 1968), p. 93.

2. Claude Lévi-Strauss, *The Savage Mind*, trans. by George Weidenfeld and Nicolson Ltd. (Chicago: University of Chicago Press, 1966), p. 24.

Selected Bibliography

PRIMARY SOURCES

Tolkien, J. R. R. *The Fellowship of the Ring: Being the First Part of The Lord of the Rings*. London: Allen and Unwin, 1954.
———. *The Hobbit: Or There and Back Again*. London: Allen and Unwin, 1937.
———. *Letters of J. R. R. Tolkien*. Edited by Humphrey Carpenter, with Christopher Tolkien. London: Allen and Unwin, 1981; reissued with new index by Wayne G. Hammond and Christina Scull, London: HarperCollins, 1999.
———. *The Monsters and the Critics and other Essays*. Edited by Christopher Tolkien London: Allen and Unwin, 1983.
———. *The Return of the King: Being the Third Part of The Lord of the Rings*. London: Allen and Unwin, 1955.
———. *The Silmarillion*. J. R. R. Tolkien. Christopher Tolkien, ed. London: Allen and Unwin, 1977.
———. *The Tolkien Reader*. New York: Ballantine, 1966.
———. *The Two Towers: Being the Second Part of The Lord of the Rings*. Edited by Christopher Tolkien, London: Allen and Unwin, 1954.
Tolkien, J. R. R., and E. V. Gordon, eds. *Sir Gawain and The Green Knight*. Oxford: Clarendon Press, 1925.
———. *Unfinished Tales of Númenor and Middle-earth*. Edited by Christopher Tolkien, London: Allen and Unwin, 1980.

The History of Middle-earth (12-volume series edited by Christopher Tolkien)

Tolkien, J. R. R. *The Book of Lost Tales, Part I*. Vol. 1. London: Allen and Unwin, 1983.
———. *The Book of Lost Tales, Part II*. Vol. 2. London: Allen and Unwin, 1984.
———. *The Lays of Beleriand*. Vol. 3. London: Allen and Unwin, 1985.
———. *The Shaping of Middle-earth*. Vol. 4. London: Allen and Unwin, 1986.
———. The Lost Road and Other Writings. Vol. 5. London: Unwin Hyman, 1987.
———. *The Return of the Shadow*. Vol. 6. London: Unwin Hyman, 1988.
———. *The Treason of Isengard*. Vol. 7. London: Unwin Hyman, 1989.
———. *The War of the Ring*. Vol. 8. London: Unwin Hyman, 1990.
———. *Sauron Defeated: The End of the Third Age*. Vol. 9. London: HarperCollins, 1992.
———. *Morgoth's Ring: The Later Silmarillion*. Vol. 10. London: HarperCollins, 1993.
———. *The War of the Jewels: The Later Silmarillion, Part II*. Vol. 11. London: HarperCollins, 1994.
———. *The Peoples of Middle-earth*. Vol. 12. London: HarperCollins, 1996.

SECONDARY SOURCES

Agøy, Nils Ivar, ed. *Between Faith and Fiction: Tolkien and the Powers of His World.* Proceedings of the Arda Symposium at the Second Northern Tolkien Festival, Oslo, August 1997. The Arda Society, Oslo, 1998.

Attebery, Brian. *Strategies of Fantasy.* Bloomington: Indiana University Press, 1992.

Auden, W. H. "At the End of the Quest, Victory." *New York Times Book Review,* January 22, 1956, 5.

———. "Good and Evil in the Lord of the Rings." *Critical Quarterly* 10 (1968): 138–42.

———. "A World Imaginary, but Real." *Encounter* 3 (November 1954): 59–62.

Battarbee, K. J., ed. *Scholarship and Fantasy.* Proceedings of The Tolkien Phenomenon, May 1992, Turku, Finland. University of Turku, 1993.

Bruner, Jerome. "Myth and Identity." In *Myth and Mythmaking,* ed. Henry A. Murray. Boston: Beacon Press, 1968.

Campbell, Joseph. *The Hero with a Thousand Faces.* New York: Pantheon Books, 1949.

———. *The Masks of God.* 4 vols. New York: Viking Press, 1959–68.

———. *The Mythic Image.* Princeton, N.J.: Princeton University Press, 1974.

———. *Myths, Dreams, and Religion.* New York: E. P. Dutton, 1970.

———. *Myths to Live By.* New York: Viking Press, 1972.

———. *The Power of Myth, with Bill Moyers.* New York: Doubleday, 1988.

Castell, Daphne. "The Realms of Tolkien." *New Worlds* 50 (November 1966): 143–54.

Chance, Jane. *The Lord of the Rings: The Mythology of Power.* New York: Twayne, 1992.

Clark, George, and Daniel Timmons, eds. *J. R. R. Tolkien and His Literary Resonances: Views of Middle-earth.* Westport, Conn.: Greenwood Press, 2000.

Collins, David R. *J. R. R. Tolkien, Master of Fantasy.* Minneapolis: Lerner Publications, 1992.

Crabbe, Kathryn F. *J. R. R. Tolkien.* New York: Frederick Ungar, 1981; revised and expanded edition, Ungar, 1988.

Crawford, Edward. *Some Light on Middle-earth.* Oxford, U.K.: Tolkien Society, 1985.

Curry, Patrick. *Defending Middle-earth.* Rev. Ed. London: HarperCollins, 1998.

Day, David. *Tolkien's Ring.* London: HarperCollins, 1994.

Dundes, Alan. Introduction to *Morphology of the Folktale,* by V. Propp. Trans. Laurence Scott. 2nd ed. Austin: University of Texas Press, 1968.

———. *The Study of Folklore.* Englewood Cliffs, N.J.: Prentice-Hall, 1965.

Flieger, Verlyn. *A Question of Time: J. R. R. Tolkien's Road to Faerie.* Kent, Ohio: Kent State University Press, 1997.

———. *Splintered Light: Logos and Language in Tolkien's World.* Grand Rapids, Mich.: Eerdmans, 1983.

Flieger, Verlyn, and Carl F. Hostetter, eds. *Tolkien's Legendarium: Essays on The History of Middle-earth.* Westport, Conn.: Greenwood Press, 2000.

Foster, Robert. *The Complete Guide to Middle-earth: From "The Hobbit" to "The Silmarillion."* New York: Ballantine Books, 1978.

Frye, Northrup. *Fables of Identity.* New York: Harcourt, Brace and World, 1961.

Green, William H. *The Hobbit: A Journey into Maturity.* New York: Twayne, 1995.

Hammond, Wayne G. *J. R. R. Tolkien: A Descriptive Bibliography.* Assisted by Douglas A. Anderson. Winchester, U.K.: St. Paul's Bibliographies, 1993.

Hein, Rolland. *Christian Mythmakers: Lewis, L'Engle, Tolkien and Others.* Chicago: Cornerstone Press, 1998.

Helms, Randel. *Tolkien and the Silmarils.* London: Thames and Hudson, 1981.

———. *Tolkien's World.* Boston: Houghton Mifflin, 1974.

Helms, Philip W., et al. *Peace and Conflict Studies in J. R. R. Tolkien's Middle-earth.* Vols. 1 and 2. Flint, Mich.: American Tolkien Society, 1994, 1999.

Honegger, Thomas, ed. *Root and Branch: Approaches Towards Understanding Tolkien.* Zurich: Walking Tree Publishers, 1999.

Irwin, W. R. "There and Back Again: The Romances of Williams, Lewis, and Tolkien." *Sewanee Review* 69 (October–December 1961): 566–78.

Isaacs, Neil D., and Rose A. Zimbardo, eds. *Tolkien: New Critical Perspectives.* Lexington: University Press of Kentucky, 1981.

Johnson, Judith A., ed. *J. R. R. Tolkien: Six Decades of Criticism.* Bibliographies and Indexes in World Literature, no. 6. Westport, Conn.: Greenwood Press, 1986.

Knight, Gareth. *The Magical World of the Inklings: J. R. R. Tolkien, C. S. Lewis, Charles Williams, Owen Barfield.* Longmead: Element Books, 1990.

Kocher, Paul H. *Master of Middle-earth: The Fiction of J. R. R. Tolkien.* Boston: Houghton Mifflin, 1972.

Lévi-Strauss, Claude. "The Structural Study of Myth." *Journal of American Folklore* 68 (1955): 428–44.

Lobdell, Jared, ed. *A Tolkien Compass.* La Salle, Ill.: Open Court Publishing 1975. New York: Ballantine Books, 1980.

———. "Words That Sound Like Castles." *National Review* September 5, 1967, 972, 974.

Miesel, Sandra L. "Some Motifs and Sources for LOTR." *Riverside Quarterly* 3 (March 1968): 125–28.

———. "Some Religious Aspects of LOTR." *Riverside Quarterly* 3 (August 1968): 209–13.

Neimark, Anne E. *Myth Maker: J. R. R. Tolkien.* San Diego: Harcourt Brace, 1996.

Nitzsche, Jane Chance. *Tolkien's Art: A Mythology for England.* London: Macmillan, 1979.

Noel, Ruth S. *The Mythology of Middle-earth.* Boston: Houghton Mifflin, 1977; London: Thames and Hudson, 1977.

O'Neill, Timothy R. *The Individuated Hobbit: Jung, Tolkien and the Archetypes of Middle-earth.* Boston: Houghton Mifflin, 1979.

Pearce, Joseph, ed. *Tolkien—A Celebration: Collected Writings on a Literary Legacy.* London: Fount, 1999.

———. *Tolkien: Man and Myth.* London: HarperCollins, 1998.

Provost, William. "Language and Myth in the Fantasy Writings of J. R. R. Tolkien." *Modern Age*, 33.1 (1990): 62–52.

Purtill, Richard L. *J. R. R. Tolkien: Myth, Morality and Religion*. San Francisco: Harper & Row, 1984.

Rank, Otto. *The Myth of the Birth of the Hero*. Translated by F. Robbins and Ely Jelliffe Smith. New York: Robert Brunner, 1952.

Reaver, J. Russell, and George W. Boswell. *Fundamentals of Folk Literature*. Oosterhout, The Netherlands: Anthropological Publications, 1962; distributed in U.S. by Humanities Press, 1969.

Reynolds, Patricia, and Glen H. GoodKnight, eds. *Proceedings of the J. R. R. Tolkien Centenary Conference, Keble College, Oxford, 1992*. Milton Keynes, U.K.: Tolkien Society; Altadena, Calif.: Mythopoeic Society, 1995.

Reynolds, Trevor, ed. *The First and Second Ages: The 5th Tolkien Society Workshop*. London: Tolkien Society, 1992.

Rosebury, Brian. *Tolkien: A Critical Assessment*. London: St. Martin's Press, 1992.

Ryan, J. S. "German Mythology Applied: The Extension of the Literary Folk Memory." *Folklore* 77 (spring 1966): 45–59.

Shippey, T. A. *J. R. R. Tolkien: Author of the Century*. Boston: Houghton Mifflin, 2001.

———. *The Road to Middle-earth*. London: Allen and Unwin, 1982.

Slochower, Harry. *Mythopoesis: Mythic Patterns in the Literary Classics*. Detroit: Wayne State University Press, 1970.

Stevens, David, and Carol D. *J. R. R. Tolkien: The Art of the Myth-maker*. San Bernardino, Calif.: Borgo Press, 1993.

Sullivan, C. W. "Tolkien and the Telling of a Traditional Narrative." *Journal of the Fantastic in the Arts* 7.1 (1996): 75–82.

"The Tolkien Papers." *Mankato Studies in English* (Mankato State College), no. 2. (February 1967).

Torkelson, Lucile. "Return of the Hero." *Milwaukee Sentinel*, November 8, 1967, 1, 4.

Tyler, J. E. A. *The Tolkien Companion*. New York: Gramercy, 2000.

Van Gennep, Arnold. *The Rites of Passage*. Translated by Monika B. Vizedom and Gabrielle L. Caffee. Chicago: University of Chicago Press, 1960.

West, Richard C. *Tolkien Criticism: An Annotated Checklist. Rev. Ed.* Kent, Ohio: Kent State University Press, 1991.

Index